Intentionally blank as was the original edition.

Plate I.

LEONARDO DA VINCI.

1452–1519.

From a drawing in red chalk by himself. In the Royal Library, Turin.

No. 1.

The
Aeronautical
Annual.

1895.

DEVOTED TO THE ENCOURAGEMENT OF EXPERIMENT WITH
AERIAL MACHINES, AND TO THE ADVANCEMENT
OF THE SCIENCE OF AERODYNAMICS.

EDITED BY

JAMES MEANS.

This publication will be sent, postpaid, to any
address on receipt of one dollar.

BOSTON, MASS.:
W. B. CLARKE & CO.,
340 WASHINGTON STREET.

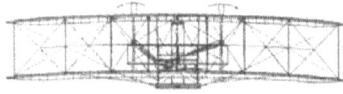

American Aeronautical Archives

Published by Markowski International Publishers
One Oakglade Circle, Hummelstown, PA 17036
American Aeronautical Archives is an imprint of
Markowski International Publishers
www.AeronauticalPublishers.com

This Markowski edition is an unabridged facsimile of the original work,
compiled and edited by James Means, and first published in 1895 then in
2003 in Celebration of the Centennial of Flight. It includes all the original
aeronautical photographs and illustrations. The Foreword to the Markowski
Edition was specially prepared for this edition.

Publisher's Cataloguing-in-Publication

Means, James, Editor, 1853-1920
    The Aeronautical Annual 1895: Foreword by Michael A. Markowski, p.cm.
    Originally published in Boston, Massachusetts by W.B. Clarke & Co., 1895
    ISBN: 978-0-938716-95-2

    1.   Flying Machine—History.   2. Aeronautics—History
    I.   Title

Manufactured in the United States of America

IF this compilation should happily bring any new workers into the field of aeronautical experiment, the hopes of the editor will be amply fulfilled.

To ask questions of Mother Nature is delectable.

If her answers be often non-committal, even such are lures to lead us into better questioning.

This number of THE ANNUAL contains not much that is new, but divers things which — to use the words of an old compiler — "do now for their Excellency and Scarceness deserve to be Reprinted."

FOREWORD

The Aeronautical Annuals of 1895-96-97 are among the most important pre-Wright era aviation books ever published. Prized by collectors, original editions are extremely rare; a pristine original set could be worth $3,000. In tribute to the brave early aviation pioneers, I am delighted to re-publish these treasures and make them available to everyone.

In a letter to James Means's son, Philip, dated November 12, 1921, Orville Wright wrote: "*The Aeronautical Annuals* of 1895-96-97 contained the best collection of reprints from the work of the earlier experimenters in aviation…, and I do not know of a better collection today. Your father showed rare good judgment in his selections, separating most of the good work from the mass of worthless matter which had been published.

"Your father's work was of great benefit to us, and I think of my personal acquaintance with him with affection."

After stumbling upon an original set of these amazing books in 1972 in an old, out-of-the-way bookstore in Boston, with Tom Peghiny, my first student and great friend ever since, I committed to advancing ultralight aviation. Tom went on to become a world champion hangglider pilot, maker of ultralight aircraft, and founder of light sport aircraft leader Flight Design USA. These three books, along with Otto Lilienthal's landmark *Birdflight as the Basis of Aviation,* inspired me to leave my job as an aerospace engineer to design and manufacture hanggliders. I then wrote *The Hang Glider's Bible*, and started publishing books.

In 1899 the Smithsonian recommended the *Annuals* to Wilbur Wright when he wrote asking for information on human flight. These three volumes are books of vision, featuring the plans, dreams, and schemes of some of aviation's visionaries—Da Vinci, Cayley, Henson, Langley, Maxim, Herring, Chanute, Lilienthal, and others.

The *Annuals* provided the Wrights with a wealth of knowledge about the thinking and experiments which had been done up until that time, giving them a foundation on which to formulate their own ideas. Each volume is packed with incredible information, drawings, and photographs of the pre-Wright era, making them must-reads for all aviation enthusiasts.

Blue skies and tailwinds,
— *Mike Markowski*

CONTENTS.

LIST OF PLATES.

NOTE OF ACKNOWLEDGMENTS.

For the articles by Thomas Walker and F. H. Wenham the editor is indebted to the Reports of the Aeronautical Society of Great Britain, for the years 1877 and 1866 respectively. (See Bibliography, p. 136.) Mr. Wenham's paper was first reprinted in the United States in the Report of the Smithsonian Institution for the year 1890.

Plates II. to VII., inclusive, are photo-engraved from " Saggio Delle Opere di Leonardo da Vinci. Tratti dal Codice Atlantico." Milan, 1872.

The illustration on the cover is made from " Astra Castra." (See Bibliography, p. 135.) The compiler of that work states that his plate is taken from one of Picard's illustrations in " The Temple of the Muses," 1730.

Plate XIV. and the small cuts on pages 134 and 139 are also taken from " Astra Castra."

The Frontispiece is from "The Literary Works of Leonardo da Vinci," by Jean Paul Richter, Ph.D. 2 vols. London, 1883.

LEONARDO DA VINCI.

THE story which tells of the sad fate of Icarus is but one of many which may be found in the pages of antiquity showing that from time immemorial man has longed to fly. Yet, these tales are but traditions, and, search as we may, no written records of the study of the great problem of flight are to be found until we come to the manuscripts of Leonardo da Vinci, who died three hundred and seventy-five years ago.

Within the limits of these pages it is only possible to give a few fragments concerning the life and works of this great man.

He was born in 1452, at the Castle Vinci, which is situated in the vale of the Arno, midway between Pisa and Florence.

Richter says, " He was the natural son of Ser Piero Antonio da Vinci, notary to the Signory of Florence. His mother's name was Caterina. The son was brought up entirely in his father's house. Of his youthful education we are unable to judge; we only know it to have been a varied one. Vasari tells us that ' in arithmetic he made such rapid progress that he often confounded the master who was teaching him by the perpetual doubts he started, and by the difficulty of the questions he proposed. He also commenced the study of music and resolved to acquire the art of playing the lute, when, being by nature of an exalted imagination and full of the most graceful vivacity, he sang to that instrument most divinely, improvising, at the same time, both the verses and the music.'

" Yet, of his early pursuits, drawing and modelling in clay had the greatest charm for him. It was this which induced his father to place him with his friend, Andrea del Verrocchio, in whose studio the boy's genius would be developed by a thorough artistic training. No more fitting teacher could at that time have been found in Florence.   Verrocchio was one of her greatest geniuses."

Sidney Colvin says, " Considering the range of his speculative as well as that of his practical powers, he seems certainly the man whose genius has the best right to be called universal of any that have ever lived.   In the fine arts he was the most accomplished painter of his generation and one of the most accomplished of the world, a distinguished sculptor, architect, and musician, and a luminous and pregnant critic."

Dr. John William Draper wrote: [1]   "Before the heliocentric theory could be developed and made to furnish a clear exposition of the solar system, which is obviously the first step to just views of the universe, it was necessary that the science of mechanics should be greatly improved — indeed, it might be said, created; for during those dreary ages following the establishment of Byzantine power, nothing had been done toward the acquisition of correct views either in statics or dynamics.   It was impossible that Europe, in her lower states of life, could produce men capable of commencing where Archimedes had left off.   She had to wait for the approach of her Age of Reason for that.   The man of capacity at last came.   Leonardo da Vinci was born. The historian Hallam, enumerating some of his works, observes, ' His knowledge was almost preternatural.'   Many of his writings still remain unpublished.   Long before Bacon he laid down the maxim that experience and observation must be the foundation of all reasoning in science; that experiment is the only interpreter of nature, and is essential to the ascertainment of laws.   Unlike Bacon, who was ignorant of mathematics and even disparaged them, he points out their supreme advantage.

" Seven years after the voyage of Columbus, this great man — great at once as an artist, mathematician, and engineer — gave a clear exposition of the theory of forces obliquely applied on a lever; a few years later he was well acquainted with the earth's annual motion.   He knew the laws of friction, subsequently demonstrated by Amontons, and the principle of virtual veloci-

---

[1] " The Intellectual Development of Europe."   Vol. II. p. 268.

Plate II.

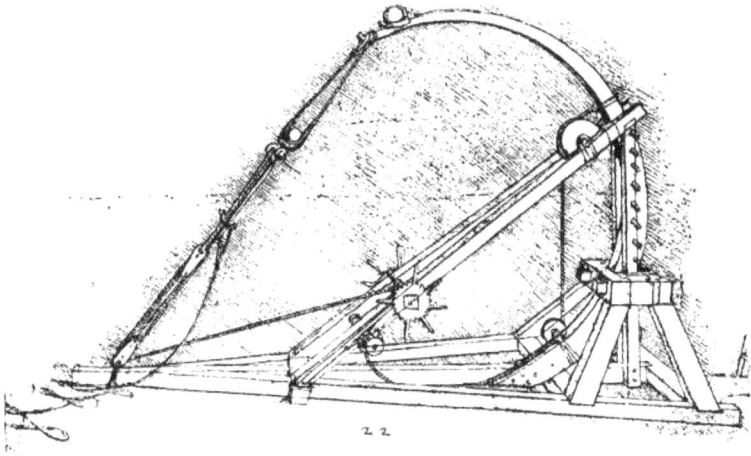

MANGONEL.

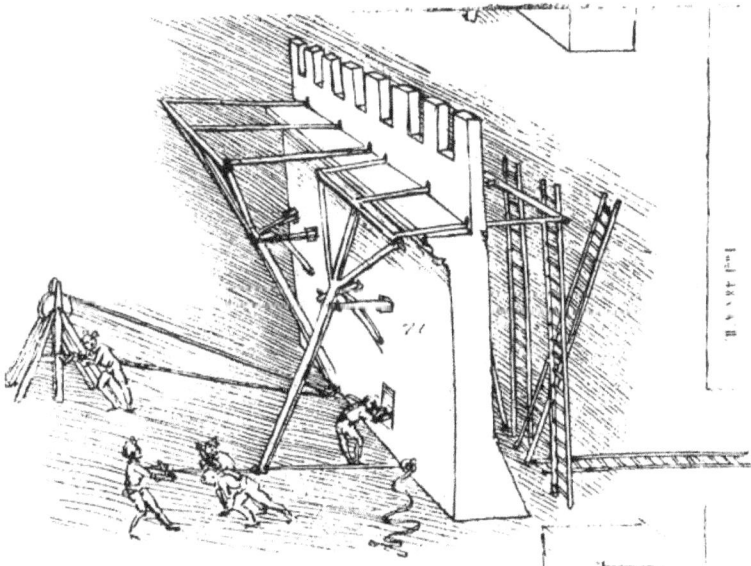

DEVICE FOR DISLODGING AN ASSAILANT'S SCALING-LADDERS.

REPRODUCTIONS OF MECHANICAL DRAWINGS BY LEONARDO DA VINCI.

Intentionally blank as was the original edition.

ties; he described the camera obscura before Baptista Porta, understood aerial perspective, the nature of colored shadows, the use of the iris, and the effects of the duration of visible impressions on the eye. He wrote well on fortification, anticipated Cartelli on hydraulics, occupied himself with the fall of bodies on the hypothesis of the earth's rotation, treated of the times of descent along inclined planes and circular arcs, and of the nature of machines. He considered, with singular clearness, respiration and combustion, and foreshadowed one of the great hypotheses of geology, the elevation of continents."

To what these writers have given may be added the statement that Leonardo was a deep student of anatomy, and a designer of flying-machines.

We may read Leonardo's own description of his accomplishments in a letter of which the manuscript is still extant. His allusion to his ability in painting is likely to arrest the attention of the reader. The date of the letter is uncertain. He settled down at Milan about 1482. The letter is addressed to Ludovico Sforza, called Il Moro. Mrs. Heaton, one of the biographers of Leonardo, rightly observes that this letter could only have been written by a genius or by a fool. It reads as follows:

" Having, most illustrious lord, seen and duly considered the experiments of all those who repute themselves masters in the art of inventing instruments of war, and having found that their instruments differ in no way from such as are in common use, I will endeavor, without wishing to injure any one else, to make known to your Excellency certain secrets of my own; as briefly enumerated here below:

" 1. I have a way of constructing very light bridges, most easy to carry, by which the enemy may be pursued and put to flight. Others also of a stronger kind, that resist fire or assault, and are easy to place and to remove. I know ways also for burning and destroying those of the enemy.

" 2. In case of investing a place, I know how to remove the water from ditches, and to make various scaling ladders, and other such instruments.

" 3. Item: If, on account of the height or strength of

position, the place cannot be bombarded, I have a way for ruining every fortress which is not on stone foundations.

"4.   I can also make a kind of cannon, easy and convenient to transport, that will discharge inflammable matters, causing great injury to the enemy and also great terror from the smoke.

" 5.   Item: By means of narrow and winding underground passages made without noise, I can contrive a way for passing under ditches or any stream.

"6.   Item: I can construct covered carts, secure and inde-structible, bearing artillery, which, entering among the enemy, will break the strongest body of men, and which the infantry can follow without any impediment.

" 7.   I can construct cannon, mortars, and fire-engines of beautiful and useful shape, and different from those in common use.

" 8.   When the use of cannon is impracticable, I can replace them by catapults, mangonels, and engines for discharging mis-siles of admirable efficacy, and hitherto unknown; in short, ac-cording as the case may be, I can contrive endless means of offence.

" 9.   And, if the fight should be at sea, I have numerous engines of the utmost activity, both for attack and defence; vessels that will resist the heaviest fire; also powders or vapors.

" 10.   In time of peace, I believe I can equal any one in architecture, and in constructing buildings, public or private, and in conducting water from one place to another.

" Then I can execute sculpture, whether in marble, bronze, or terra-cotta; also in painting I can do as much as any other, be he who he may.

" Further, I could engage to execute the bronze horse in last-ing memory of your father, and of the illustrious house of Sforza, and, if any of the above-mentioned things should ap-pear impossible and impracticable to you, I offer to make trial of them in your park, or in any other place that may please your Excellency, to whom I commend myself in utmost hu-mility."

Leonardo left not less than five thousand pages of manu-

Plate III.

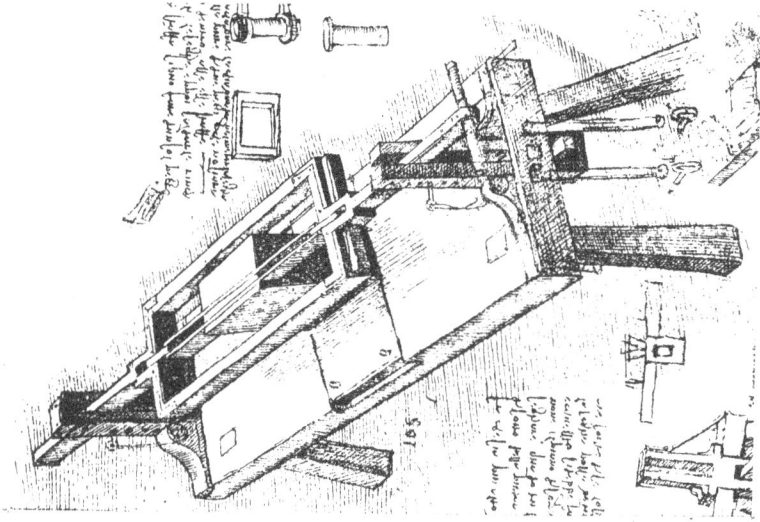

MACHINE FOR SAWING A BLOCK OF MARBLE INTO SLABS.

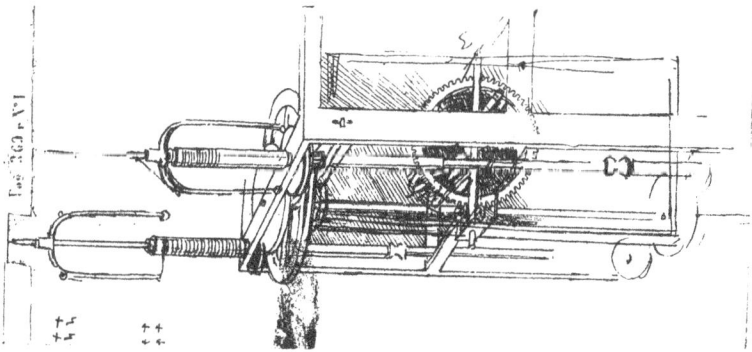

SPINNING MACHINE?

REPRODUCTIONS OF MECHANICAL DRAWINGS BY LEONARDO DA VINCI.

Intentionally blank as was the original edition.

Plate IV.

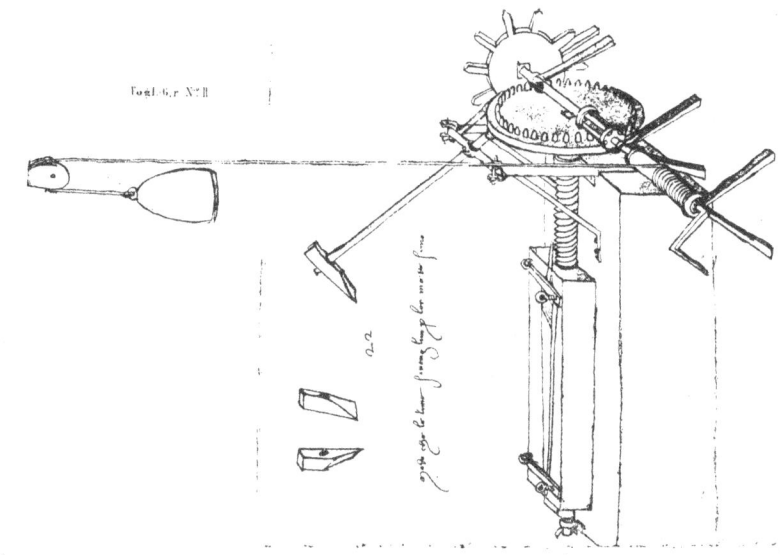

MACHINE FOR CUTTING FILES.

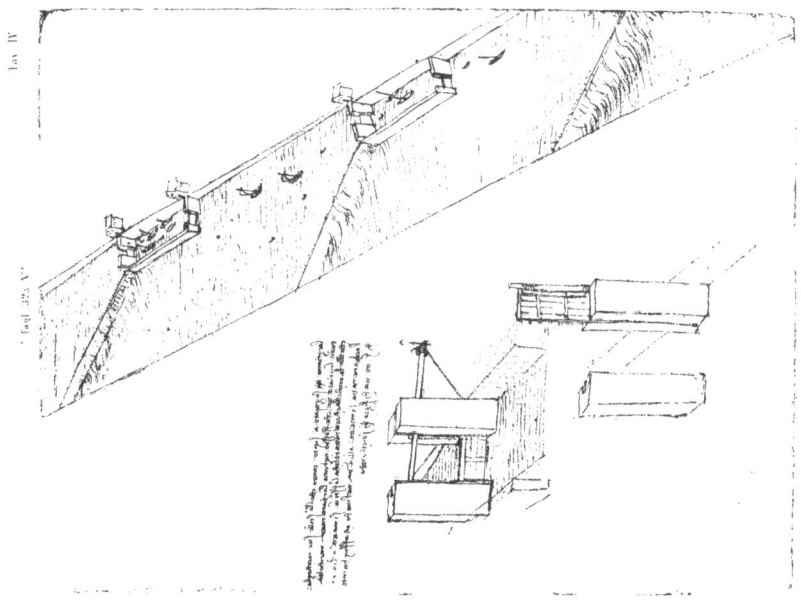

CANAL—LOCKS AND GATES FOR THE SAME.

REPRODUCTIONS OF MECHANICAL DRAWINGS BY LEONARDO DA VINCI.

Intentionally blank as was the original edition.

Plate V.

Tav. XI

Fogl. 378 r. N° 1

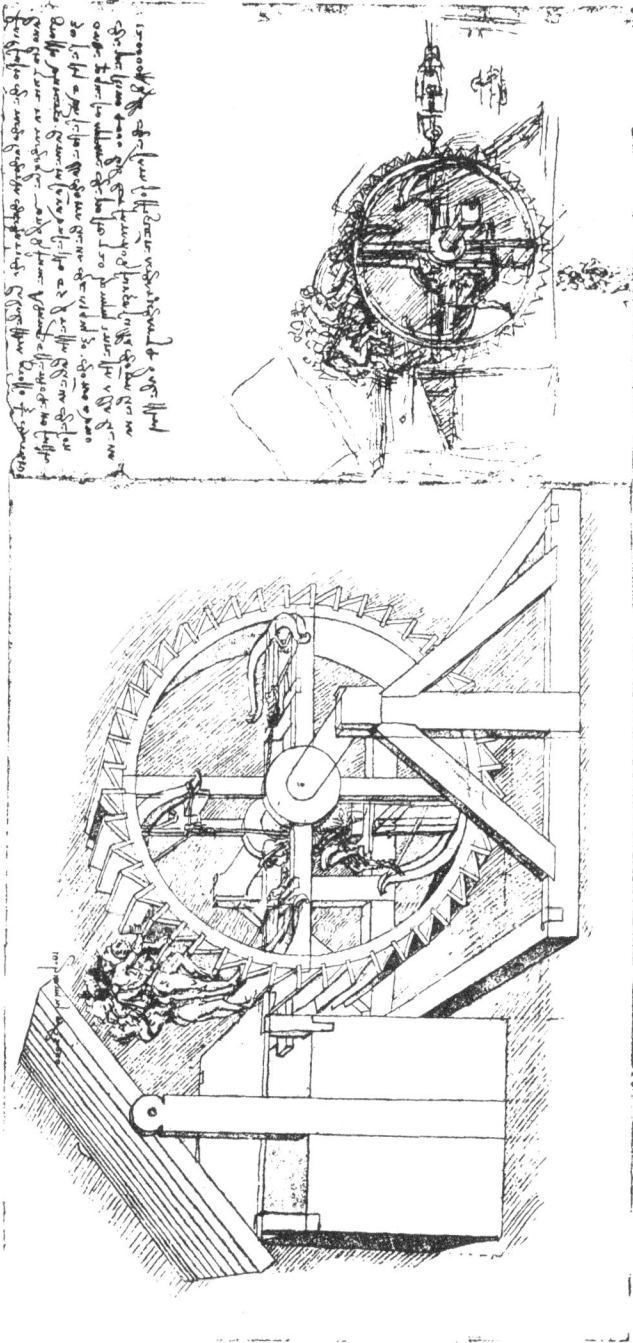

This may be one of the machines which Leonardo, in his letter to Sforza, refers to as "engines for discharging missiles of admirable efficacy, and hitherto unknown." Its action seems to be as follows: The men who furnish the motive power are protected from the missiles of the enemy by the sloping barrier; the four cross-bows inside are drawn by the operator, who causes the line attached to each bow-string to bind upon the immovable axle. At the right moment the bow is released, and sends the projectile through the opening under the platform. The drawing at the right seems to give an impression of the engine in the heat of action.

REPRODUCTIONS OF MECHANICAL DRAWINGS BY LEONARDO DA VINCI.

Intentionally blank as was the original edition.

script, which are preserved to this day. The work of editing and publishing these is now going on. One of the most recent publications is entitled "*Codice sul volo degli uccelli.*" ("Treatise upon the Flight of Birds.")[1] Other volumes are shortly to follow. These will contain the unpublished manuscripts preserved in England, some in the British, others in the South Kensington Museum, and the remainder in the Royal Library at Windsor.

Dr. Jean Paul Richter compiled and edited from original manuscripts, "The Literary Works of Leonardo da Vinci." A two-volume edition was published in London in 1883.

The greater part of Leonardo's manuscripts are written with the left hand from right to left, so that a mirror gives the true form of the letters.

Dr. Richter says, "Leonardo's literary labors in various departments, both of art and of science, were those essentially of an enquirer; hence the analytical method is that which he employs in arguing out his investigations and dissertations. The vast structure of his scientific theories is consequently built up of numerous separate researches, and it is much to be lamented that he should never have collated and arranged them. His love for detailed research — as it seems to me — was the reason that in almost all the manuscripts the different paragraphs appear to us to be in utter confusion. On one and the same page, observations on the most dissimilar subjects follow each other without any connection. A page, for instance, will begin with some principles of astronomy, or the motion of the earth; then come the laws of sound, and finally some precepts as to color. Another page will begin with his investigations on the structure of the intestines, and end with philosophical remarks as to the relations of poetry to painting; and so forth.

"Leonardo himself lamented this confusion, and for that reason I do not think that the publication of the texts in the order in which they occur in the originals would at all fulfil his intentions. No reader could find his way through such a labyrinth; Leonardo himself could not have done it.

.   .   .   .

----

[1] Edoardo Rouveyre, Editore. Paris, 1893.

"The beginning of Leonardo's literary labors dates from about his thirty-seventh year, and he seems to have carried them on without any serious interruption till his death. Thus the manuscripts that remain represent a period of about thirty years. Within this space of time his handwriting altered so little that it is impossible to judge from it of the date of any particular text. The exact dates, indeed, can only be assigned to certain note-books, in which the year is incidentally indicated, and in which the order of the leaves has not been altered since Leonardo used them.

.   .   .   .

"There can be no doubt that in more than one department his principles and discoveries were infinitely more in accord with the teachings of modern science than with the views of his contemporaries. For this reason his extraordinary gifts and merits are far more likely to be appreciated in our own time than they could have been during the preceding centuries. He has been unjustly accused of having squandered his powers, by beginning a variety of studies, and then, having hardly begun, throwing them aside. The truth is, that the labors of three centuries have hardly sufficed for the elucidation of some of the problems which occupied his mighty mind.

"Alexander von Humboldt has borne witness that 'he was the first to start on the road towards the point where all the impressions of our senses converge in the idea of the unity of nature.' Nay, yet more may be said. The very words which are inscribed on the monument of Alexander von Humboldt himself, at Berlin, are perhaps the most appropriate in which we can sum up our estimate of Leonardo's genius: '*Majestati naturae par ingenium.*'"

The master died in France in the year 1519.

Plate VI.

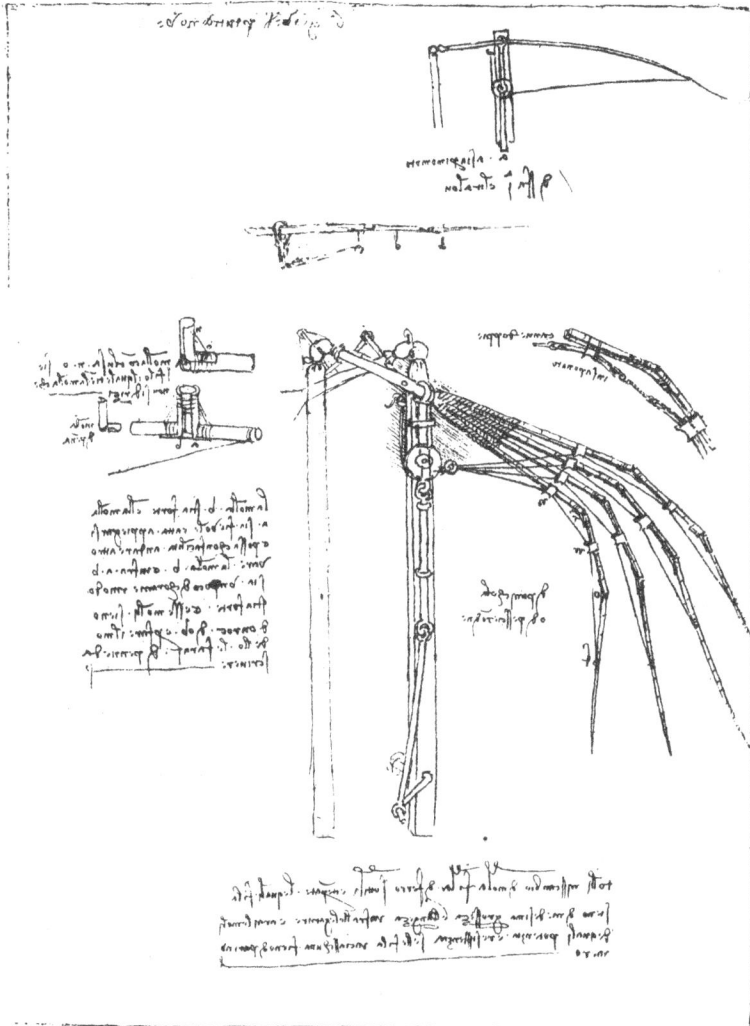

DESIGN FOR MECHANICAL WING.

REPRODUCTIONS OF MECHANICAL DRAWINGS BY LEONARDO DA VINCI.

Intentionally blank as was the original edition.

Plate VII.

STUDIES OF VARIOUS PROBLEMS CONCERNING FLIGHT.

REPRODUCTION OF DRAWINGS AND MANUSCRIPT BY LEONARDO DA VINCI.

Intentionally blank as was the original edition.

FROM LEONARDO'S "TREATISE UPON THE FLIGHT OF BIRDS."

Those feathers which are farthest from their fastening will be the most flexible; then the tops of the feathers of the wings will be always higher than their origins, so that we may with reason say, that the bones of the wings will be lower in the lowering of the wings than any other part of the wings, and in the raising these bones of the wing will always be higher than any other part of such a wing. Because the heaviest part always makes itself the guide of the movement.

The kite and other birds which beat their wings little, go seeking the course of the wind, and when the wind prevails on high then they will be seen at a great height, and if it prevails low they will hold themselves low.

When the wind does not prevail in the air, then the kite beats its wings several times in its flight in such a way that it raises itself high and acquires a start, with which start, descending afterwards a little, it goes a long way without beating its wings, and when it is descended it does the same thing over again, and so it does successively, and this descent without flapping the wings serves it as a means of resting itself in the air after the aforesaid beating of the wings.

When a bird which is in equilibrium throws the centre of resistance of the wings behind the centre of gravity, then such a bird will descend with its head down.

This bird which finds itself in equilibrium shall have the centre of resistance of the wings more forward than the bird's centre of gravity, then such a bird will fall with its tail turned to the earth.

When the bird is in the position and wishes to rise it will raise its shoulders and the air will press between its sides and the point of the wings so that it will be condensed and will give the bird the movement toward the ascent and will produce a momentum in the air, which momentum of the air will by its condensation push the bird up.

———————

Of four movements performed by birds reflected and incidental to different aspects of the wind.

The slanting descent of birds being made against the wind will be made under the wind, and its reflex movement will be made above the wind. But if such an incidental movement is made to the east, the wind blowing from the north, then the northern wing will remain under the wind; in the reflex movement will do the same, so that, at the end of this reflex the bird will find itself with its face to the north.

And if the bird descends to the south, the northern wind reigning, he will make such a descent above the wind and his reflex movement will be under the wind; but here comes in a long dispute which will be told in its place, because here it seems to happen that he cannot make the reflex movement.

When the bird makes his reflex movement above the wind then he will mount much more than belongs to his natural momentum, seeing that he adds to that the help of the wind which, entering under him, acts as a wedge. But when he has reached the end of the ascent he will have used up his momentum, and he will have remaining only the help of the wind, which would overturn him because he strikes it with his breast, were it not that he lowers the right or left wing, which makes him turn to the right or to the left descending in a semi-circle.

———————

The descent of the bird will always be by that extremity which shall be the nearest to its centre of gravity. The heaviest part of the bird which descends will remain always in front of the centre of its mass.

Plate VIII.

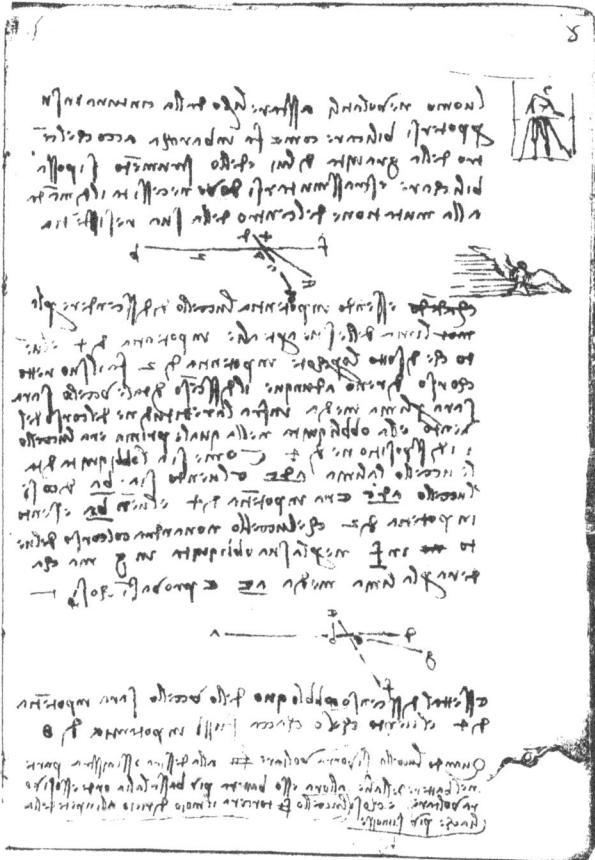

FROM LEONARDO'S TREATISE ON THE FLIGHT OF BIRDS.

Paris, 1893.

REPRODUCTION OF DRAWINGS AND MANUSCRIPT BY LEONARDO DA VINCI.

Intentionally blank as was the original edition.

Plate IX.

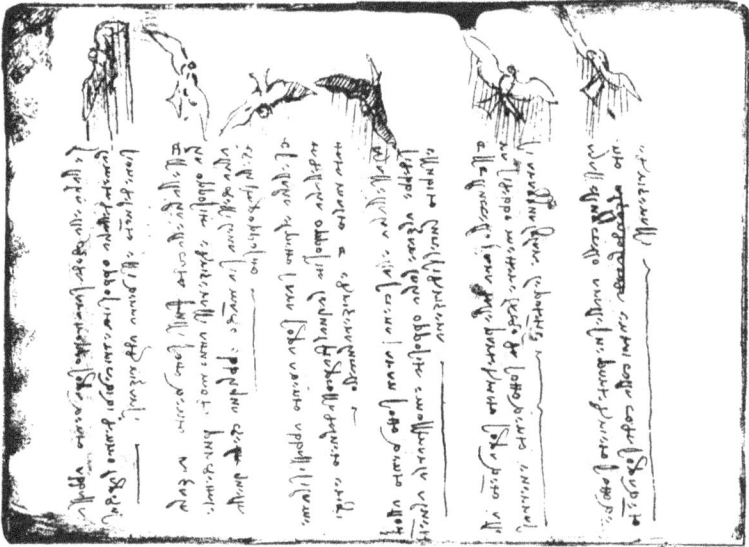

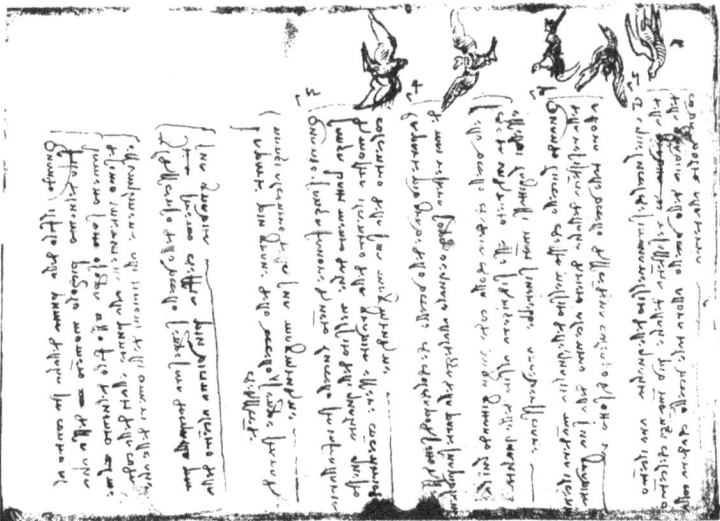

FROM LEONARDO'S TREATISE ON THE FLIGHT OF BIRDS,
Paris, 1893.

REPRODUCTION OF DRAWINGS AND MANUSCRIPT BY LEONARDO DA VINCI.

Intentionally blank as was the original edition.

When without help of the wind the bird remains in the air without flapping its wings, this shows that the centre of its gravity is concentric with the centre of its mass.

———

The man in the flying-machine to be free from the waist up that he may be able to keep himself in equilibrium as he does in a boat, so that the centre of his gravity and that of the instrument may set itself in equilibrium and change when necessity requires it to the changing of the centre of its resistance.

NOTE. — This paragraph refers to the figure of the man seen in Plate VIII. Of course a supporting surface above the man is presupposed. The interval between Leonardo's writing and Lilienthal's practical work is nearly four hundred years. The former has clearly shown that he understood the supporting power of aerocurves, and in this last paragraph he indicates a knowledge of the fact that the chief difficulty which a soaring man encounters is that of keeping his centre of gravity at all times in the right place. To appreciate Leonardo one must understand Lilienthal. See Mr. Chanute's "Progress in Flying-Machines," p. 285, line 30; and p. 286, line 1. — *Ed.*

ON AERIAL NAVIGATION.

(*From Nicholson's Journal, November, 1809.*)

BY SIR GEORGE CAYLEY, BART.

BROMPTON, Sept. 6, 1809.

SIR, I observed in your Journal for last month, that a watch-maker at Vienna, of the name of Degen, has succeeded in raising himself in the air by mechanical means. I waited to receive your present number, in expectation of seeing some farther account of this experiment, before I commenced transcribing the following essay upon aerial navigation, from a number of memoranda which I have made at various times upon this subject. I am induced to request your publication of this essay, because I conceive, that, in stating the fundamental principles of this art, together with a considerable number of facts and practical observations, that have arisen in the course of much attention to this subject, I may be expediting the attainment of an object, that will in time be found of great importance to mankind; so much so, that a new æra in society will commence, from the moment that aerial navigation is familiarly realized.

It appears to me, and I am more confirmed by the success of the ingenious Mr. Degen, that nothing more is necessary, in order to bring the following principles into common practical use, than the endeavours of skilful artificers, who may vary the means of execution, till those most convenient are attained.

Since the days of Bishop Wilkins the scheme of flying by artificial wings has been much ridiculed; and indeed the idea of attaching wings to the arms of a man is ridiculous enough, as the pectoral muscles of a bird occupy more than two-thirds of its whole muscular strength, whereas in man the muscles, that could operate upon wings thus attached, would probably

(16)

not exceed one-tenth of his whole mass. There is no proof that, weight for weight, a man is comparatively weaker than a bird; it is therefore probable, if he can be made to exert his whole strength advantageously upon a light surface similarly proportioned to his weight as that of the wing to the bird, that he would fly like the bird, and the ascent of Mr. Degen is a sufficient proof of the truth of this statement.

The flight of a strong man by great muscular exertion, though a curious and interesting circumstance, in as much as it will probably be the first means of ascertaining this power, and supplying the basis whereon to improve it, would be of little use. I feel perfectly confident, however, that this noble art will soon be brought home to man's general convenience, and that we shall be able to transport ourselves and families, and their goods and chattels, more securely by air than by water, and with a velocity of from 20 to 100 miles per hour.

To produce this effect, it is only necessary to have a first mover, which will generate more power in a given time, in proportion to its weight, than the animal system of muscles.

The consumption of coal in a Boulton and Watt's steam engine is only about $5\frac{1}{2}$ lbs. per hour for the power of one horse. The heat produced by the combustion of this portion of inflammable matter is the sole cause of the power generated; but it is applied through the intervention of a weight of water expanded into steam, and a still greater weight of cold water to condense it again. The engine itself likewise must be massy enough to resist the whole external pressure of the atmosphere, and therefore is not applicable to the purpose proposed. Steam engines have lately been made to operate by expansion only, and those might be constructed so as to be light enough for this purpose, provided the usual plan of a large boiler be given up, and the principle of injecting a proper charge of water into a mass of tubes, forming the cavity for the fire, be adopted in lieu of it. The strength of vessels to resist internal pressure being inversely as their diameters, very slight metallic tubes would be abundantly strong, whereas a large boiler must be of great substance to resist a strong pressure. The following estimate will show the probable weight of such an engine with its charge for one hour.

	lb.
The engine itself from 90 to	100
Weight of inflamed cinders in a cavity presenting about 4 feet surface of tube	25
Supply of coal for one hour	6
Water for ditto, allowing steam of one atmosphere to be $\frac{1}{1800}$ the specific gravity of water	32
	163

I do not propose this statement in any other light than as a rude approximation to truth, for as the steam is operating under the disadvantage of atmospheric pressure, it must be raised to a higher temperature than in Messrs. Boulton and Watt's engine; and this will require more fuel; but if it take twice as much, still the engine would be sufficiently light, for it would be exerting a force equal to raising 550 lb. one foot high per second, which is equivalent to the labour of six men, whereas the whole weight does not much exceed that of one man.

It may seem superfluous to inquire farther relative to first movers for aerial navigation; but lightness is of so much value in this instance, that it is proper to notice the probability that exists of using the expansion of air by the sudden combustion of inflammable powders or fluids with great advantage. The French have lately shown the great power produced by igniting inflammable powders in close vessels; and several years ago an engine was made to work in this country in a similar manner, by the inflammation of spirit of tar. I am not acquainted with the name of the person who invented and obtained a patent for this engine, but from some minutes with which I was favoured by Mr. William Chapman, civil engineer in Newcastle, I find that 80 drops of the oil of tar raised eight hundred weight to the height of 22 inches; hence a one horse power many consume from

10 to 12 pounds per hour, and the engine itself need not exceed 50 pounds weight. I am informed by Mr. Chapman, that this engine was exhibited in a working state to Mr. Rennie, Mr. Edmund Cartwright, and several other gentlemen, capable of appreciating its powers; but that it was given up in consequence of the expense attending its consumption being about eight times greater than that of a steam engine of the same force.

Probably a much cheaper engine of this sort might be produced by a gas-light apparatus, and by firing the inflammable air generated, with a due portion of common air, under a piston. Upon some of these principles it is perfectly clear, that force can be obtained by a much lighter apparatus than the muscles of animals or birds, and therefore in such proportion may aerial vehicles be loaded with inactive matter. Even the expansion steam engine doing the work of six men, and only weighing equal to one, will as readily raise five men into the air, as Mr. Degen can elevate himself by his own exertions; but by increasing the magnitude of the engine, 10, 50, or 500 men may equally well be conveyed; and convenience alone, regulated by the strength and size of materials, will point out the limit for the size of vessels in aerial navigation.

Having rendered the accomplishment of this object probable upon the general view of the subject, I shall proceed to point out the principles of the art itself. For the sake of perspicuity I shall, in the first instance, analyze the most simple action of the wing in birds, although it necessarily supposes many previous steps. When large birds, that have a considerable extent of wing compared with their weight, have acquired their full velocity, it may frequently be observed, that they extend their wings, and without waving them, continue to skim for some time in a horizontal path. Fig. 1, in the Plate, represents a bird in this act.

Let a b be a section of the plane of both wings opposing the horizontal current of the air (created by its own motion) which may be represented by the line c d, and is the measure of the velocity of the bird. The angle *b d c* can be increased at the will of the bird, and to preserve a perfectly horizontal path, without the wing being waved, must continually be increased in a complete ratio, (useless at present to enter into) till the motion is stopped altogether; but at one given time the position of the wings may be truly represented by the angle *b d c*. Draw *d e* perpendicular to the plane of the wings, produce the line *e d* as far as required, and from the point *e*, assumed at pleasure in the line *d e*, let fall *e f* perpendicular to *d f*. Then *d e* will represent the whole force of the air under the wing; which being resolved into the two forces *e f* and *f d*, the former represents the force that sustains the weight of the bird, the latter the retarding force by which the velocity of the motion, producing the current *c d*, will continually be diminished. *e f* is always a known quantity, being equal to the weight of the bird, and hence *f d* is also known, as it will always bear the same proportion to the weight of the bird, as the sine of the angle *b d e* bears to its cosine, the angles *d e f*, and *b d c*, being equal. In addition to the retarding force thus received is the direct resistance, which the bulk of the bird opposes to the current. This is a matter to be entered into separately from the principle now under consideration; and for the present may be wholly neglected, under the supposition of its being balanced by a force precisely equal and opposite to itself.

Before it is possible to apply this basis of the principle of flying in birds to the purposes of aerial navigation, it will be necessary to encumber it with a few practical observations. The whole problem is confined within these limits, viz. To make a surface support a given weight by the application of power to the resistance of air. Magnitude is the first question respecting the surface. Many experiments have been made upon the direct resistance of air, by Mr. Robins, Mr. Rouse, Mr. Edgeworth, Mr. Smeaton, and others. The result of Mr. Smeaton's experiments and observations was, that a surface of a square foot met with a resistance of one pound, when it travelled perpendicularly to itself through air at a velocity of 21

Nicholson's Philos Journal Vol.XXIV. Pl. 6 p.74

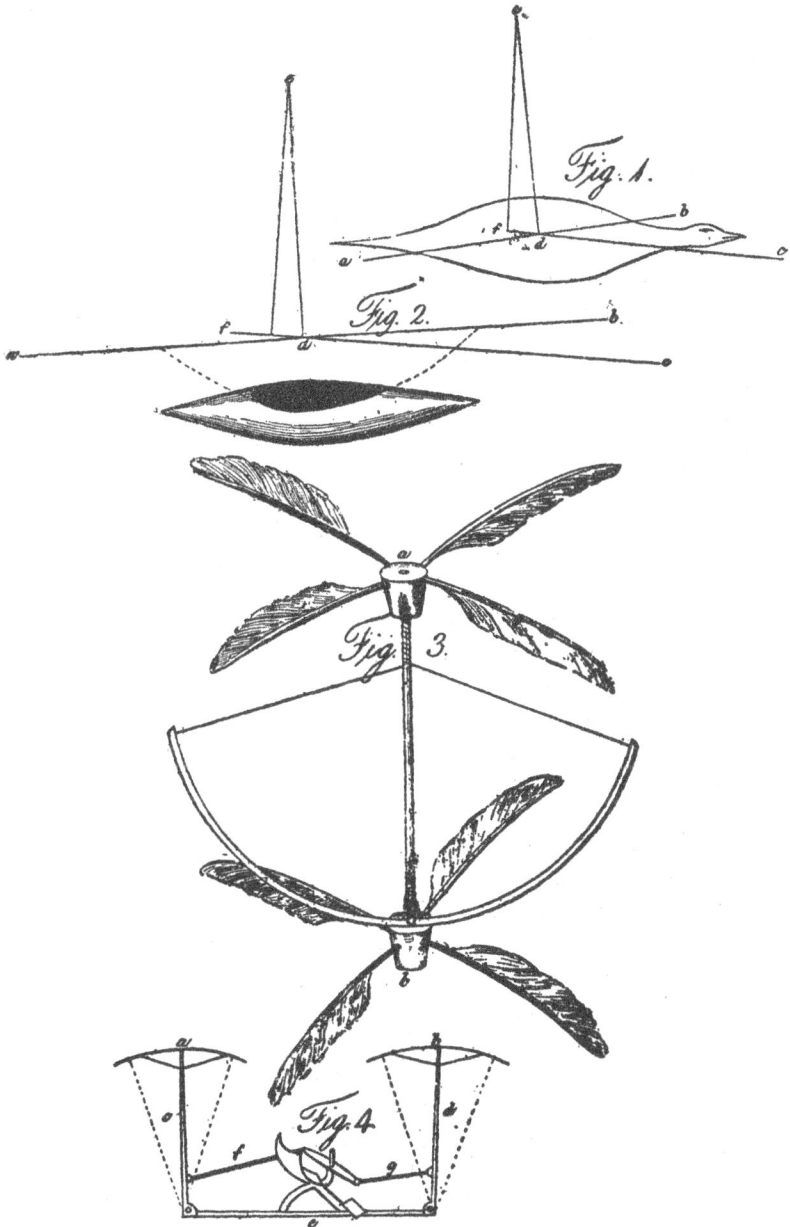

Fig. 1.

Fig. 2.

Fig. 3.

Fig. 4.

feet per second. I have tried many experiments upon a large
scale to ascertain this point. The instrument was similar to
that used by Mr. Robins, but the surface used was larger,
being an exact square foot, moving round upon an arm about
five feet long, and turned by weights over a pulley. The time
was measured by a stop watch, and the distance travelled over
in each experiment was 600 feet. I shall for the present only
give the result of many carefully repeated experiments, which
is, that a velocity of 11.538 feet per second generated a resistance of 4 ounces; and that a velocity of 17.16 feet per second
gave 8 ounces resistance. This delicate instrument would have
been strained by the additional weight necessary to have tried
the velocity generating a pressure of one pound per square foot;
but if the resistance be taken to vary as the square of the
velocity, the former will give the velocity necessary for this purpose at 23.1 feet, the latter 24.28 per second. I shall therefore
take 23.6 feet as somewhat approaching the truth.

Having ascertained this point, had our tables of angular resistance been complete, the size of the surface necessary for
any given weight would easily have been determined. Theory,
which gives the resistance of a surface opposed to the same
current in different angles, to be as the squares of the sine of
the angle of incidence, is of no use in this case; as it appears
from the experiments of the French Academy, that in acute
angles, the resistance varies much more nearly in the direct
ratio of the sines, than as the squares of the sines of the angles
of incidence.   The flight of birds will prove to an attentive
observer, that, with a concave wing apparently parallel to the
horizontal path of the bird, the same support, and of course
resistance, is obtained. And hence I am inclined to suspect,
that, under extremely acute angles, with concave surfaces, the
resistance is nearly similar in them all. I conceive the operation may be of a different nature from what takes place in larger
angles, and may partake more of the principle of pressure exhibited in the instrument known by the name of the hydrostatic paradox, a slender filament of the current is constantly
received under the anterior edge of the surface, and directed

upward into the cavity, by the filament above it, in being obliged to mount along the convexity of the surface, having created a slight vacuity immediately behind the point of separation. The fluid accumulated thus within the cavity has to make its escape at the posterior edge of the surface, where it is directed considerably downward; and therefore has to overcome and displace a portion of the direct current passing with its full velocity immediately below it; hence whatever elasticity this effort requires operates upon the whole concavity of the surface, excepting a small portion of the anterior edge. This may or may not be the true theory, but it appears to me to be the most probable account of a phenomenon, which the flight of birds proves to exist.

Six degrees was the most acute angle, the resistance of which was determined by the valuable experiments of the French Academy; and it gave $\frac{4}{10}$ of the resistance, which the same surface would have received from the same current when perpendicular to itself. Hence then a superficial foot, forming an angle of six degrees with the horizon, would, if carried forward horizontally (as a bird in the act of skimming) with a velocity of 23.6 feet per second, receive a pressure of $\frac{4}{10}$ of a pound perpendicular to itself. And, if we allow the resistance to increase as the square of the velocity, at 27.3 feet per second it would receive a pressure of one pound. I have weighed and measured the surface of a great many birds, but at present shall select the common rook (*corvus frugilegus*) because its surface and weight are as nearly as possible in the ratio of a superficial foot to a pound. The flight of this bird, during any part of which they can skim at pleasure, is (from an average of many observations) about 34.5 feet per second. The concavity of the wing may account for the greater resistance here received, than the experiments upon plain surfaces would indicate. I am convinced, that the angle made use of in the crow's wing is much more acute than six degrees; but in the observations, that will be grounded upon these data, I may safely state, that every foot of such curved surface, as will be used in aerial navigation, will receive a resistance of one pound, perpendicular to itself, when carried through the air in an angle of six degrees with the line of its path, at a velocity of about 34 or 35 feet per second.

Let *a b*, fig. 2, represent such a surface or sail made of thin cloth, and containing about 200 square feet (if of a square form the side will be a little more than 14 feet) ; and the whole of a firm texture. Let the weight of the man and the machine be 200 pounds. Then if a current of wind blew in the direction *c d*, with a velocity of 35 feet per second, at the same time that a cord represented by *c d* would sustain a tension of 21 pounds, the machine would be suspended in the air, or at least be within a few ounces of it (falling short of such support only in the ratio of the sine of the angle of 94 degrees compared with radius; to balance which defect, suppose a little ballast to be thrown out) for the line *d e* represents a force of 200 pounds, which, as before, being resolved into *d f* and *f e*, the former will represent the resistance in the direction of the current, and the latter that which sustains the weight of the machine. It is perfectly indifferent whether the wind blow against the plane, or the plane be driven with an equal velocity against the air. Hence, if this machine were pulled along by a cord *c d*, with a tension of about 21 pounds, at a velocity of 35 feet per second, it would be suspended in a horizontal path; and if in lieu of this cord any other propelling power were generated in this direction, with a like intensity, a similar effect would be produced. If therefore the waft of surfaces advantageously moved, by any force generated within the machine, took place to the extent required, aerial navigation would be accomplished. As the acuteness of the angle between the plane and current increases, the propelling power required is less and less. The principle is similar to that of the inclined plane, in which theoretically one pound may be made to sustain all but an infinite quantity; for in this case, if the magnitude of the surface be increased ad infinitum, the angle with the current may be diminished, and consequently the propelling force, in the same ratio. In practice, the extra resistance of the car and other parts of the machine, which consume a considerable portion of power, will regulate the limits to which this principle, which is the true basis of aerial navigation, can be carried; and the perfect ease with which some birds are suspended in long horizontal flights, without one waft of their wings, encourages the idea, that a slight power only is necessary.

As there are many other considerations relative to the practical introduction of this machine, which would occupy too much space for any one number of your valuable Journal, I propose, with your approbation, to furnish these in your subsequent numbers; taking this opportunity to observe, that perfect steadiness, safety, and steerage, I have long since accomplished upon a considerable scale of magnitude; and that I am engaged in making some farther experiments upon a machine I constructed last summer, large enough for aerial navigation, but which I have not had an opportunity to try the effect of, excepting as to its proper balance and security. It was very beautiful to see this noble white *bird* sail majestically from the top of a hill to any given point of the plane below it, according to the set of its rudder, merely by its own weight, descending in an angle of about 18 degrees with the horizon. The exertions of an individual, with other avocations, are extremely inadequate to the progress, which this valuable subject requires. Every man acquainted with experiments upon a large scale well knows how leisurely fact follows theory, if ever so well founded. I do therefore hope, that what I have said, and have still to offer, will induce others to give their attention to this subject; and that England may not be backward in rivalling the continent in a more worthy contest than that of arms.

As it may be an amusement to some of your readers to see a machine rise in the air by mechanical means, I will conclude my present communication by describing an instrument of this kind, which any one can construct at the expense of ten minutes labour.

a and *b*, fig. 3, are two corks, into each of which are inserted four wing feathers from any bird, so as to be slightly inclined like the sails of a windmill, but in opposite directions in each set. A round shaft is fixed in the cork *a*, which ends in a sharp point. At the upper part of the cork *b* is fixed a whalebone bow, having a small pivot hole in its centre, to receive the point of the shaft. The bow is then to be strung equally on each side to the upper portion of the shaft, and the little machine is completed. Wind up the string by turning the flyers different ways, so that the spring of the bow may unwind them with their anterior edges ascending; then place the cork with the bow attached to it upon a table, and with a finger on the upper cork press strong enough to prevent the string from unwinding, and taking it away suddenly, the instrument will rise to the ceiling. This was the first experiment I made upon this subject in the year 1796. If in lieu of these small feathers large planes, containing together 200 square feet, were similarly placed, or in any other more convenient position, and were turned by a man, or first mover of adequate power, a similar effect would be the consequence, and for the mere purpose of ascent this is perhaps the best apparatus; but speed is the great object of this invention, and this requires a different structure.

P. S. In lieu of applying the continued action of the inclined plane by means of the rotative motion of flyers, the same principle may be made use of by the alternate motion of surfaces backward and forward; and although the scanty description hitherto published of Mr. Degen's apparatus will scarcely justify any conclusion upon the subject; yet as the principle above described must be the basis of every engine for aerial navigation by mechanical means, I conceive, that the method adopted by him has been nearly as follows. Let A and B, fig. 4, be two surfaces or parachutes, supported upon the long shafts C and D, which are fixed to the ends of the connecting beam E, by hinges. At E, let there be a convenient seat for the aeronaut, and before him a cross bar turning upon a pivot in its centre, which being connected with the shafts of the parachutes by the rods F and G, will enable him to work them alternately backward and forward, as represented by the dotted lines. If the upright shafts be elastic, or have a hinge to give way a little near their tops, the weight and resistance of the parachutes will incline them so, as to make a small angle with the direction of their motion, and hence the machine rises. A slight heeling of the parachutes toward one side, or an alteration in the position of the weight, may enable the aeronaut to steer such an apparatus tolerably well; but many better constructions may be formed, for combining the requisites of speed, convenience and steerage. It is a great point gained, when the first experiments demonstrate the practicability of an art; and Mr. Degen, by whatever means he has effected this purpose, deserves much credit for his ingenuity.

ON AERIAL NAVIGATION.

(*From Nicholson's Journal, February, 1810.*)

BY SIR GEORGE CAYLEY, BART.

HAVING, in my former communication, described the general principle of support in aerial navigation, I shall proceed to show how this principle mu'st be applied, so as to be steady and manageable.

Several persons have ventured to descend from balloons in what is termed a parachute, which exactly resembles a large umbrella, with a light car suspended by cords underneath it.

Mr. Garnerin's descent in one of these machines will be in the recollection of many; and I make the remark for the purpose of alluding to the continued oscillation, or want of steadiness, which is said to have endangered that bold aeronaut. It is very remarkable, that the only machines of this sort, which have been constructed, are nearly of the worst possible form for producing a steady descent, the purpose for which they are intended. To render this subject more familiar, let us recollect, that in a boat, swimming upon water, its stability or stiffness depends, in general terms, upon the *weight* and distance from the centre of the section elevated above the water, by any given heel of the boat, on one side; and on the *bulk*, and its distance from the centre, which is immersed below the water, on the other side; the combined endeavour of the one to fall, and of the other to swim, produces the desired effect in a well-constructed boat. The centre of gravity of the boat being more or less below the centre of suspension is an additional cause of its stability.

Let us now examine the effect of a parachute represented by A B, Fig. 1, Pl. III. When it has heeled into the position *a b*, the side *a* is become perpendicular to the current, created by the descent, and therefore resists with its greatest power; whereas

(28)

Nicholson's Philos. Journal. Vol.XXV. pl.III. p.81.

Sir G. Cayley, on Aerial Navigation.

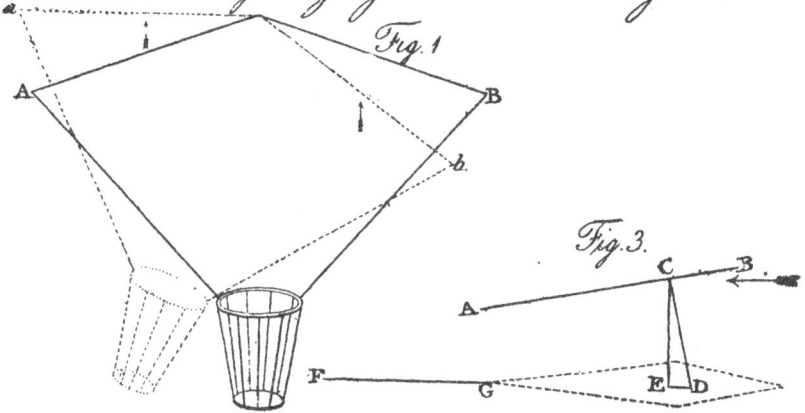

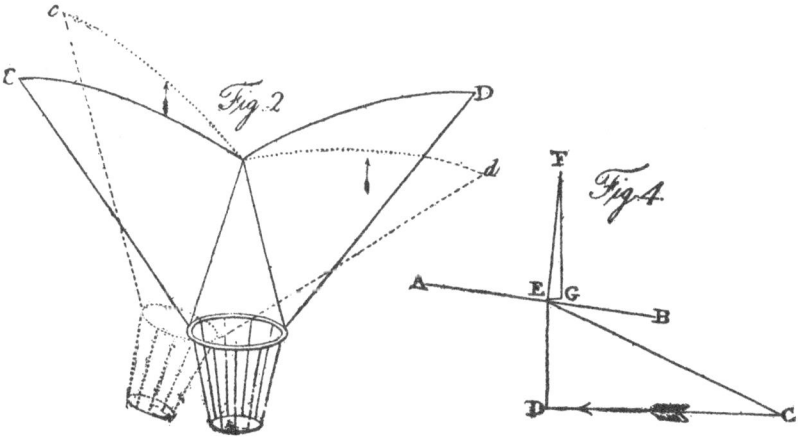

Fig. 1

Fig. 2

Fig. 3.

Fig. 4.

the side *b* is become more oblique, and of course its resistance is
much diminished.   In the instance here represented, the angle
of the parachute itself is 144°, and it is supposed to heel 18°,
the comparative resistance of the side *a* to the side *b*, will be as
the square of the line *a*, as radius, to the square of the sine
of the angle of *b* with the current; which, being 54 degrees,
gives the resistances nearly in the ratio of 1 to 0.67; and this
will be reduced to only 0.544, when estimated in a direction perpendicular to the horizon.   Hence, so far as this form of the sail
or plane is regarded, it operates directly in opposition to the
principle of stability; for the side that is required to fall resists
much more in its new position, and that which is required to
rise resists much less; therefore complete inversion would be
the consequence, if it were not for the weight being suspended
so very much below the surface, which, counteracting this tendency, converts the effort into a violent oscillation.

On the contrary, let the surface be applied in the inverted
position, as represented at C D, Fig. 2, and suppose it to be
heeled to the same angle as before, represented by the dotted
lines *c d*.   Here the exact reverse of the former instance takes
place; for that side, which is required to rise, has gained resistance by its new position, and that which is required to sink has
lost it; so that as much power operates to restore the equilibrium in this case, as tended to destroy it in the other: the
operation very much resembling what takes place in the common boat.[1]

This angular form, with the apex downward, is the chief basis
of stability in aerial navigation; but as the sheet which is to
suspend the weight attached to it, in its horizontal path through
the air, must present a slightly concave surface in a small angle
with the current, this principle can only be used in the lateral
extension of the sheet; and this most effectually prevents any
rolling of the machine from side to side.   Hence, the section of

[1] A very simple experiment will show the truth of this theory. Take a circular piece of
writing paper, and folding up a small portion, in the line of two radii, it will be formed into
an obtuse cone. Place a small weight in the apex, and letting it fall from any height, it
will steadily preserve that position to the ground. Invert it, and, if the weight be fixed, like
the life boat, it rights itself instantly.

the inverted parachute, Fig. 2, may equally well represent the cross section of a sheet for aerial navigation.

The principle of stability in the direction of the path of the machine, must be derived from a different source. Let A B, Fig. 3, be a longitudinal section of a sail, and let C be its centre of resistance, which experiment shows to be considerably more forward than the centre of the sail. Let C D be drawn perpendicular to A B, and let the centre of gravity of the machine be at any point in that line, as at D. Then, if it be projected in a horizontal path with velocity enough to support the weight, the machine will retain its relative position, like a bird in the act of skimming; for, drawing C E perpendicular to the horizon, and D E parallel to it, the line C E will, at some particular moment, represent the supporting power, and likewise its opponent the weight; and the line D E will represent the retarding power, and its equivalent, that portion of the projectile force expended in overcoming it: hence, these various powers being exactly balanced, there is no tendency in the machine but to proceed in its path, with its remaining portion of projectile force.

The stability in this position, arising from the centre of gravity being below the point of suspension, is aided by a remarkable circumstance, that experiment alone could point out. In very acute angles with the current it appears, that the centre of resistance in the sail does not coincide with the centre of its surface, but is considerably in front of it. As the obliquity of the current decreases, these centres approach, and coincide when the current becomes perpendicular to the sail. Hence any heel of the machine backward or forward removes the centre of support behind or before the point of suspension; and operates to restore the original position, by a power, equal to the whole weight of the machine, acting upon a lever equal in length to the distance the centre has removed.

To render the machine perfectly steady, and likewise to enable it to ascend and descend in its path, it becomes necessary to add a rudder in a similar position to the tail in birds. Let F G be the section of such a surface, parallel to the current; and let it be capable of moving up and down upon G, as a centre, and of being fixed in any position. The powers of the machine being previously balanced, if the least pressure be exerted by the current, either upon the upper or under surface of the rudder, according to the will of the aeronaut, it will cause the machine to rise or fall in its path, so long as the projectile or propelling force is continued with sufficient energy. From a variety of experiments upon this subject I find, that, when the machine is going forward with a superabundant velocity, or that which would induce it to rise in its path, a very steady horizontal course is effected by a considerable depression of the rudder, which has the advantage of making use of this portion of sail in aiding the support of the weight. When the velocity is becoming less, as in the act of alighting, then the rudder must gradually recede from this position, and even become elevated, for the purpose of preventing the machine from sinking too much in front, owing to the combined effect of the want of projectile force sufficient to sustain the centre of gravity in its usual position, and of the centre of support approaching the centre of the sail.

The elevation and depression of the machine are not the only purposes, for which the rudder is designed. This appendage must be furnished with a vertical sail, and be capable of turning from side to side, in addition to its other movements, which effects the complete steerage of the vessel.

All these principles, upon which the support, steadiness, elevation, depression, and steerage, of vessels for aerial navigation, depend, have been abundantly verified by experiments both upon a small and a large scale. Last year I made a machine, having a surface of 300 square feet, which was accidentally broken before there was an opportunity of trying the effect of the propelling apparatus; but its steerage and steadiness were perfectly proved, and it would sail obliquely downward in any direction, according to the set of the rudder. Even in this state, when any person ran forward in it, with his full speed, taking advantage of a gentle breeze in front, it would bear upward so strongly as scarcely to allow him to touch the ground; and would frequently lift him up, and convey him several yards together.

The best mode of producing the propelling power is the only thing, that remains yet untried toward the completion of the invention. I am preparing to resume my experiments upon this subject, and state the following observations, in the hope that others may be induced to give their attention towards expediting the attainment of this art.

The act of flying is continually exhibited to our view; and the principles upon which it is effected are the same as those before stated. If an attentive observer examines the waft of a wing, he will perceive, that about one third part, toward the extreme point, is turned obliquely backward; this being the only portion, that has velocity enough to overtake the current, passing so rapidly beneath it, when in this unfavourable position. Hence this is the only portion that gives any propelling force.

To make this more intelligible, let A B, Fig. 4, be a section of this part of the wing. Let C D represent the velocity of the bird's path, or the current, and E D that of the wing in its waft: then C E will represent the magnitude and direction of the compound or actual current striking the under surface of the wing. Suppose E F, perpendicular to A B, to represent the whole pressure; E G being parallel to the horizon, will represent the propelling force; and G F, perpendicular to it, the supporting power. A bird is supported as effectually during the return as during the beat of its wing; this is chiefly effected by receiving the resistance of the current under that portion of the wing next the body where its receding motion is so slow as to be of scarcely any effect. The extreme portion of the wing, owing to its velocity, receives a pressure downward and obliquely forward, which forms a part of the propelling force; and at the same time, by forcing the hinder part of the middle portion of the wing downward, so increases its angle with the current, as to enable it still to receive nearly its usual pressure from beneath.

As the common rook has its surface and weight in the ratio

of a square foot to a pound, it may be considered as a standard for calculations of this sort; and I shall therefore state, from the average of many careful observations, the movements of that bird. Its velocity, represented by C D, Fig. 4, is 34.5 feet per second. It moves its wing up and down once in flying over a space of 12.9 feet. Hence, as the centre of resistance of the extreme portion of the wing moves over a space of 0.75 of a foot each beat or return, its velocity is about 4 feet per second, represented by the line E D. As the wing certainly overtakes the current, it must be inclined from it in an angle something less than 7°, for at this angle it would scarcely be able to keep parallel with it, unless the waft downward were performed with more velocity than the return; which may be and probably is the case, though these movements appear to be of equal duration. The propelling power, represented by E G, under these circumstances, cannot be equal to an eighth part of the supporting power G F, exerted upon this portion of the wing; yet this, together with the aid from the return of the wing, has to overcome all the retarding power of the surface, and the direct resistance occasioned by the bulk of the body.

It has been before suggested, and I believe upon good grounds, that very acute angles vary little in the degree of resistance they make under a similar velocity of current. Hence it is probable, that this propelling part of the wing receives little more than its common proportion of resistance, during the waft downward. If it be taken at one-third of the whole surface, and one-eighth of this be allowed as the propelling power, it will only amount to one twenty-fourth of the weight of the bird; and even this is exerted only half the duration of the flight. The power gained in the return of the wing must be added, to render this statement correct, and it is difficult to estimate this; yet the following statement proves, that a greater degree of propelling force is obtained, upon the whole, than the foregoing observations will justify. Suppose the largest circle that can be described in the breast of a crow, to be 12 inches in area. Such a surface, moving at the velocity of 34.5 feet per second, would meet a resistance of 0.216 of a pound, which, reduced by the proportion of the resistance of a sphere to its great circle (given by Mr. Robins as 1 to 2.27) leaves a resistance of 0.095 of a pound, had the breast been hemispherical. It is probable however, that the curve made use of by Nature to avoid resistance, being so exquisitely adapted to its purpose, will reduce this quantity to one half less than the resistance of the sphere, which would ultimately leave 0.0475 of a pound as somewhat approaching the true resistance. Unless therefore the return of the wing gives a greater degree of propelling force than the beat, which is improbable, no such resistance of the body could be sustained. Hence, though the eye cannot perceive any distinction between the velocities of the beat and return of the wing, it probably exists, and experiment alone can determine the proper ratios between them.

From these observations we may, however, be justified in the remark — that the act of flying, when properly adjusted by the Supreme Author of every power, requires less exertions than, from the appearance, is supposed.

ON AERIAL NAVIGATION.

(*From Nicholson's Journal, March, 1810.*)

BY SIR GEORGE CAYLEY, BART.

BROMPTON, Dec. 6, 1809.

NOT having sufficient data to ascertain the exact degree of propelling power exerted by birds in the act of flying, it is uncertain what degree of energy may be required in this respect in vessels for aerial navigation: yet, when we consider the many hundred miles of continued flight exerted by birds of passage, the idea of its being only a small effort is greatly corroborated. To apply the power of the first mover to the greatest advantage in producing this effect, is a very material point. The mode universally adopted by nature is the oblique waft of the wing. We have only to choose between the direct beat overtaking the velocity of the current, like the oar of a boat; or one, applied like the wing, in some assigned degree of obliquity to it. Suppose 35 feet per second to be the velocity of an aerial vehicle, the oar must be moved with this speed previous to its being able to receive any resistance; then, if it be only required to obtain a pressure of $\frac{1}{10}$-th of a pound upon each square foot, it must exceed the velocity of the current 7.5 feet per second. Hence its whole velocity must be 42.5 feet per second. Should the same surface be wafted downward, like a wing, with the hinder edge inclined upward in an angle of about 50° 40′ to the current, it will overtake it at a velocity of 3.5 feet per second; and as a slight unknown angle of resistance generates a pound pressure per square foot at this velocity, probably a waft of little more than 4 feet per second would produce this effect; one tenth part of which would be the propelling power. The advantage in favour of this mode of application, compared with the former, is rather more than ten to one.

In combining the general principles of aerial navigation for the practice of the art many mechanical difficulties present themselves, which require a considerable course of skilfully applied experiments, before they can be overcome. But to a certain extent the air has already been made navigable; and no one, who has seen the steadiness with which weights to the amount of ten stone (including four stone, the weight of the machine) hover in the air, can doubt of the ultimate accomplishment of this object.

The first impediment I shall take notice of is the great proportion of power, that must be exerted previous to the machine's acquiring that velocity, which gives support upon the principle of the inclined plane; together with the total want of all support during the return of any surface used like a wing. Many birds, and particularly water fowl, run and flap their wings for several yards before they can gain support from the air. The swift (*hirundo apus Lin.*) is not able to elevate itself from level ground. The inconvenience under consideration arises from very different causes in these two instances. The supporting surface of most swimming birds does not exceed the ratio of $\frac{4}{10}$-ths of a square foot to every pound of their weight: the swift, though it scarcely weighs an ounce, measures eighteen inches in extent of wing. The want of surface in the one case, and the inconvenient length of wing in the other, oblige these birds to aid the *commencement* of their flight by other expedients; yet they can both fly with great power, when they have acquired their full velocity.

A second difficulty in aerial navigation arises from the great extent of lever, which is constantly operating against the first mover, in consequence of the distance of the centre of support in large surfaces, if applied in the manner of wings.

A third and general obstacle is the mechanical skill required to unite great extension of surface with strength and lightness of structure; at the same time having a firm and steady movement in its working parts, without exposing unnecessary obstacles to the resistance of the air. The first of these obstacles, that have been enumerated, operates much more powerfully against aerial navigation upon a large scale, than against birds;

because the small extent of their wings obliges them to employ a very rapid succession of strokes, in order to acquire that velocity which will give support; and during the small interval of the return of the wing, their weight is still rising, as in a leap, by the impulse of one stroke, till it is again aided by another. The large surfaces that aerial navigation will probably require, though necessarily moved with the same velocity, will have a proportionably longer duration both of the beat and return of the wing; and hence a greater descent will take place during the latter action, than can be overcome by the former.

There appears to be several ways of obviating this difficulty. There may be two surfaces, each capable of sustaining the weight, and placed one above the other, having such a construction as to work up and down in opposition when they are moved, so that one is always ready to descend, the moment the other ceases. These surfaces may be so made, by a valvelike structure, as to give no opposition in rising up, and only to resist in descent.

The action may be considered either oblique, as in rotative flyers; alternately so, without any up and down waft, as in the engine I have ascribed to Mr. Degen; by means of a number of small wings in lieu of large ones, upon the principle of the flight of birds, with small intervals of time between each waft; and lastly by making use of light wheels to preserve the propelling power both of the beat and the return of the wings, till it accumulates sufficiently to elevate the machine, upon the principle of those birds which run themselves up. This action might be aided by making choice of a descending ground like the swift.

With regard to another part of the first obstacle I have mentioned, viz. the absolute quantity of power demanded being so much greater at first than when the full velocity has been acquired; it may be observed, that, in the case of human muscular strength being made use of, a man can exert, for a few seconds, a surprising degree of force. He can run up stairs, for instance, with a velocity of from 6 to 8 feet perpendicular height per second, without any dangerous effort; here the muscles of his legs only are in action; but, for the sake of making a moderate statement, suppose that with the activity of his arms and body, in addition to that of his legs, he is equal to raising his weight 8 feet per second; if in this case he weighs 11 stone, or 154 pounds, he will be exerting, for the time, an energy equal to more than the ordinary force of two of Messrs. Boulton and Watt's steam horses; and certainly more than twelve men can bestow upon their constant labour.

If expansive first movers be made use of, they may be so constructed, as to be capable of doing more than their constant work; or their power may be made to accumulate for a few moments by the formation of a vacuum, or the condensation of air, so that these expedients may restore at one time, in addition to the working of the engine, that which they had previously absorbed from it.

With regard to the second obstacle in the way of aerial navigation, viz. the length of leverage to which large wing-like surfaces are exposed, it may be observed, that, being a constant and invariable quality, arising from the degree of support such surfaces give, estimated at their centres of resistance, it may be balanced by any elastic agent, that is so placed as to oppose it. Let A and B, Pl. IV, fig. 1, be two wings of an aerial vehicle in the act of skimming; then half the weight of the vessel is supported from the centre of resistance of each wing; as represented by the arrows under them. If the shorter ends of these levers be connected by cords to the string of a bow C, of sufficient power to balance the weight of the machine at the points A and B, then the moving power will be left at full liberty to produce the waft necessary to bend up the hinder edge of the wing, and gain the propelling power. A bow is not in fact an equable spring, but may be made so by using a spiral fusee. I have made use of it in this place merely as the most simple mode of stating the principle I wished to exhibit. Should a counterbalancing spring of this kind be adopted in the practice of aerial navigation, a small well polished cylinder, furnished with what may be termed a bag piston (upon the principle made use of by nature in preventing the return of the blood to the heart, when it has been driven into the aorta, by the intervention of the semilunar valves) would, by a vacuum being excited each stroke of the wing, produce the desired effect, with scarcely any loss by friction.[1]   These elastic agents may likewise be useful in gradually stopping the momentum of large surfaces when used in any alternate motion, and in thus restoring it during their return.

Another principle, that may be applied to obviate this leverage of a wing, is that of using such a construction as will make the supporting power of the air counterbalance itself.   It has been before observed, that only about one third of the wing in birds is applied in producing the propelling power; the remainder, not having velocity sufficient for this purpose, is employed in giving support, both in the beat and return of the wing.

Let A and B, fig. 2, be two wings continued beyond the pole or hinge upon which they turn at C.   If the extreme parts at A and B be long and narrow, they may be balanced, when in the act of skimming, by a broad extension of less length on their opposite sides; this broad extension, like the lower part of the wing, will always give nearly the same support, and the propelling part of the surface will be at liberty to act unincumbered by the leverage of its supporting power.   This plan may be modified many different ways; but my intention, as in the former case, is still the principle in its simplest form.

A third principle upon which the leverage of a surface may be prevented is by giving it a motion parallel to itself, either directly up and down, or obliquely so.   The surface A I, fig. 3, may be moved perpendicularly, by the shaft which supports it,

---

[1] I have made use of several of these pistons, and have no scruple in asserting, that for all blowing engines, where friction is an evil, and being very nearly airtight is sufficient, there is no other piston at all comparable with them.   The most irregular cylinder, with a piston of this kind, will act with surprising effect.   To give an instance; a cylinder of sheet tin, 8 inches long and 3½ in diameter, required 4 pounds to force the piston down in 15 minutes; and in other trials became perfectly tight in some positions, and would proceed no farther.   The friction, when the cylinder was open at both ends, did not exceed ⅛ an ounce.

Nicholsons Philos Journal. Vol. XXIV pl. IV

Sir G. Cayley on Aerial Navigation

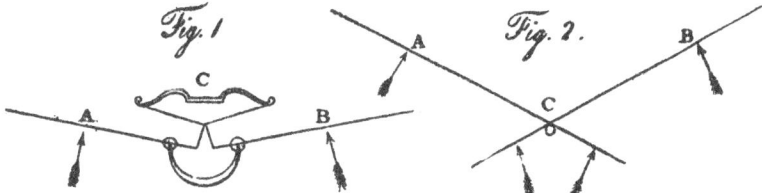

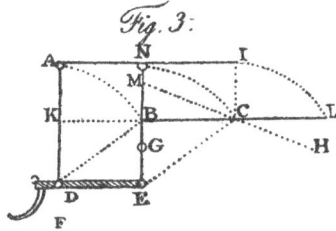

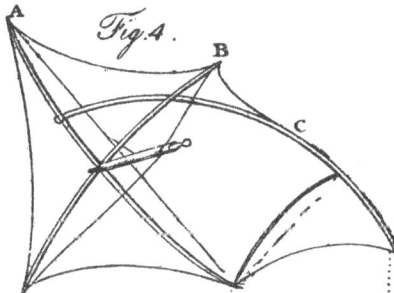

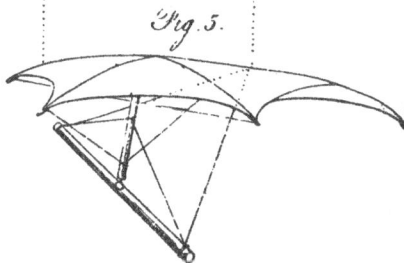

Fig. 1

Fig. 2.

Fig. 3.

Fig. 4.

Fig. 5.

down to the position K C: or, if it be supported upon two
shafts with hinges at D and E, it may be moved obliquely parallel to itself into the position B L.

A fourth principle upon which the leverage may be greatly
avoided, where only one hinge is used, is by placing it considerably below the plane of the wing, as at the point D, fig. 3, in
respect to the surface A. It may be observed in the heron,
which is a weak bird with an extended surface, that its wings
curve downward considerably from the hinge to the tip; hence
the extreme portion, which receives the chief part of the stroke,
is applied obliquely to the current it creates; and thus evades
in a similar degree the leverage of that portion of the supporting
power, which is connected with the propelling power. These
birds seldom carry their waft much below the level of the hinge
of the wing, where this principle, so far as respects the supporting power, would vanish.

By making use of two shafts of unequal length, the two last
mentioned principles may be blended to any required extent.
Suppose one hinge to be at F, and the other at G, fig. 3, then
the surface, at the extent of its beat, would be in the position
of the line H M. If the surface A I, fig. 3, be supported only
upon one shaft, N E, be capable of being forced in some degree
from its rectangular position in respect to the shaft, and be concave instead of flat as here represented; then the waft may be
used alternately backward and forward, according to the principles of the machine I have ascribed to Mr. Degen. This
construction combines the principles of counterpoising the
supporting power of one part of the surface, by that of an
opposite part, when the machine is in the act of skimming; and
likewise the advantages of the low hinge, with the principle of
leaving little or no interval without support.

All that has hitherto appeared respecting Mr. Degen's apparatus is, that it consisted of two surfaces, which were worked
by a person sitting between them. This statement communi-
cates no real information upon the subject; for scarcely any one
would attempt to fly without *two* wings; without these being
equally poised by placing the weight *between* them; and also,

without these surfaces being capable of receiving motion from his muscular action. I may be altogether mistaken in my conjecture; my only reason for ascribing this structure of mine to Mr. Degen's machine is, that, if it were properly executed upon this principle, it would be attended with success. The drawing, or rather diagram, which is given of this machine in the first part of my essay, is only for the purpose of exhibiting the principle in a form capable of being understood. The necessary bracings, etc., required in the actual execution of such a plan, would have obscured the simple nature of its action; and were therefore omitted. The plan of its movement is also simply to exhibit, in a tangible form, the possibility of effecting the intended alternate motion of the parachutes. The seat is fronted lengthwise for the purpose of accommodating the mode of communicating the movement.

A fifth mode of avoiding leverage is by using the continued action of oblique horizontal flyers, or an alternate action of the same kind, with surfaces so constructed as to accommodate their position to such alternate motion; the hinge or joint being in these cases vertical. In the construction of large vessels for aerial navigation, a considerable portion of fixed sail will probably be used; and no more surface will be allotted, towards gaining the propelling power, than what is barely necessary, with the extreme temporary exertion of the first mover, to elevate the machine and commence the flight. In this case the leverage of the fixed surface is done away.

The general difficulties of structure in aerial vehicles, (arising from the extension, lightness, and strength required in them; together with great firmness in the working parts, and at the same time such an arrangement as exposes no unnecessary obstacles to the current,) I cannot better explain than by describing a wing, which has been constructed with a view to overcome them.

Fig. 4 represents the shape of the cloth, with a perspective view of the poles upon which it is stretched with perfect tightness. Upon the point where the rods A and B intersect is erected an oval shaft; embracing the two cross poles by a slender iron fork; for the purpose of preserving their strength uninjured by boring. To this shaft are braced the ends of the pole B, so as to give this pole any required degree of curvature. The pole A is strung like a common bow to the same curve as the pole B; and is only connected with the upright shaft by what may be called a check brace; which will allow the hinder end of this pole to heel back to a certain extent, but not the fore end. The short brace producing this effect is shown in fig. 4. Fig. 5 exhibits the fellow wing to that represented in fig. 4, erected upon a beam, to which it is so braced, as to convert the whole length of it into a hinge. The four braces coming from the ends of this beam are shown: two of them terminate near the top of the centre of the other shaft; the others are inserted into the point C, fig. 4, of the bending rod. A slight bow, not more than three-eighths of an inch thick, properly curved by its string, and inserted between the hinder end of the pole A, and the curved pole C, completes the wing.

This fabrick contained 54 square feet, and weighed only eleven pounds. Although both these wings together did not compose more than half the surface necessary for the support of a man in the air, yet during their waft they lifted the weight of nine stone. The hinder edge, as is evident from the construction, being capable of giving way to the resistance of the air, any degree of obliquity, for the purpose of a propelling power, may be used.

I am the more particular in describing this wing, because it exemplifies almost all the principles that can be resorted to in the construction of surfaces for aerial navigation. Diagonal bracing is the great principle for producing strength without accumulating weight; and, if performed by thin wires, looped at their ends, so as to receive several laps of cordage, produces but a trifling resistance in the air, and keeps tight in all weathers. When bracings are well applied, they make the poles, to which are attached, bear endwise. The hollow form of the quill in birds is a very admirable structure for lightness combined with strength, where external bracings cannot be had; a tube being the best application of matter to resist as a lever; but the principle of bracing is so effectual, that, if properly applied, it will abundantly make up for the clumsiness of human invention in other respects; and should we combine both these principles, and give diagonal bracing to the tubular bamboo cane, surfaces might be constructed with a greater degree of strength and lightness, than any made use of in the wings of birds.

The surface of a heron's wing is in the ratio of 7 square feet to a pound. Hence, according to this proportion, a wing of 54 square feet would weigh about $7\frac{3}{4}$ pounds: on the contrary the wings of water fowl are so much heavier, that a surface of 54 square feet, according to their structure, will weigh $18\frac{1}{2}$ lb. I have in these instances quoted nearly the extreme cases among British birds; the wing I have described may therefore be considered as nearly of the same weight in proportion to its bulk as that of most birds.

Another principle exhibited in this wing is that of the poles being couched within the cloth, so as to avoid resistance. This is accomplished by the convexity of the frame, and the excessive lightness of the cloth. The poles are not allowed to form the edge of the wing, excepting at the extreme point of the bow, where it is very thin, and also oblique to the current. The thick part of this pole is purposely conveyed considerably within the edge. In birds, a membrane covered with feathers is stretched before the thick part of the bone of the wing, in a similar manner, and for the same purpose. The edge of the surface is thus reduced to the thickness of a small cord, that is sown to the cloth, and gives out loops whenever any fastening is required. The upright shaft is the only part that opposes much direct resistance to the current, and this is obviated in a great degree by a flat oval shape, having its longest axis parallel to the current.

The joint or hinge of this wing acts with great firmness, in consequence of its being supported by bracings to the line of its axis, and at a considerable distance from each other; in fact the bracings form the hinge.

The means of communicating motion to any surfaces must vary so much, according to the general structure of the whole machine, that I shall only observe at present, that where human muscular action is employed, the movement should be similar to the mode of pulling oars; from which any other required motion may be derived; the foot-board in front enables a man to exert his full force in this position. The wings I have described were wafted in this manner; and when they lifted with a power of 9 stone, not half of the blow, which a man's strength could have given, was exerted, in consequence of the velocity required being greater than convenient under the circumstances. Had these wings been intended for elevating the person who worked them, they should have contained from 100 to 150 square feet each; but they were constructed for the purpose of an experiment relative to the propelling power only.

Avoiding direct resistance is the next general principle, that it is necessary to discuss. Let it be remembered as a maxim in the art of aerial navigation, that every pound of direct resistance, that is done away, will support 30 pounds of additional weight without any additional power. The figure of a man seems but ill calculated to pass with ease through the air, yet I hope to prove him to the full as well made in this respect as the crow, which has hitherto been our standard of comparison, paradoxical as it may appear.

The principle, that surfaces of similar bodies increase only as the squares of their homologous lines, while their weights, or rather solid contents, increase as the cubes of those lines, furnishes the solution. This principle is unanimously in favour of large bodies. The largest circle that can be described in a crow's breast is about 12 square inches in area. If a man exposes a direct bulk of 6 square feet, the ratio of their surfaces will be as 1 to 72; but the ratio of their weight is as 1 to 110; which is $1\frac{1}{2}$ to 1 in favour of the man, provided he were within a case as well constructed for evading resistance, as the body of the crow; but even supposing him to be exposed in his natural cylindric shape, in the foreshortened posture of sitting to work his oars, he will probably receive less resistance than the crow.

It is of great importance to this art, to ascertain the real solid of least resistance, when the length or breadth is limited. Sir

Isaac Newton's beautiful theorem upon this subject is of no practical use, as it supposes each particle of the fluid, after having struck the solid, to have free egress; making the angles of incidence and reflection equal; particles of light seem to possess this power, and the theory will be true in that case; but in air the action is more like an accumulation of particles, rushing up against each other, in consequence of those in contact with the body being retarded. The importance of this subject is not less than the difficulties it presents; it affects the present interests of society in its relation to the time occupied in the voyages of ships; it will have still more effect when aerial navigation, now in its cradle, is brought home to the uses of man. I shall state a few crude hints upon this point, to which my subject has so unavoidably led, and on which I am so much interested, and shall be glad if in so doing I may excite the attention of those, who are competent to an undertaking greatly beyond my grasp.

Perhaps some approach toward ascertaining the actual solid of least resistance may be derived from treating the subject in a manner something similar to the following. Admit that such a solid is already attained (the length and width being necessarily taken at pleasure). Conceive the current intercepted or disturbed, by the largest circle that can be drawn within the given spindle, to be divided into concentric tubular laminæ of equal thickness. At whatever distance from this great circle the apex of the spindle commences, on all sides of this point the central lamina will be reflected in diverging pencils, (or rather an expanding ring,) making their angles of incidence and reflection equal. After this reflection they rush against the second lamina and displace it: this second lamina contains three times more fluid than the first; consequently each pencil in the first meets three pencils in the second; and their direction, after the union, will be one fourth of the angle, with respect to the axis, which the first reflection created. In this direction these two laminæ proceed till they are themselves reflected, when they (considered as one lamina of larger dimensions) rush against the third and fourth, which together contain three times the fluid in the two former laminæ, and thus reduce the direction of the combined mass to one fourth of the angle between the axis and the line of the second reflection.   This process is constant, whatever be the angles formed between the surface of the actual solid of least resistance at these points of reflection, and the directions of the currents thus reflected.

From this mode of reasoning, which must in some degree resemble what takes place, and which I only propose as a resemblance, it appears, that the fluid keeps creeping along the curved surface of such a solid, meeting it in very acute angles.   Hence, as the experiments of the French Academy show, that the difference of resistance between the direct impulse, and that in an angle of six degrees, on the same surface, is only in the ratio of 10 to 4, it is probable, that in the slight difference of angles that occur in this instance, the resistances may be taken as equal upon every part, without any material deviation from truth.   If this reasoning be correct, it will reduce the question, so far as utility is concerned, within a strictly abstract mathematical inquiry.

It has been found by experiment, that the shape of the hinder part of the spindle is of as much importance as that of the front, in diminishing resistance.   This arises from the partial vacuity created behind the obstructing body.   If there be no solid to fill up this space, a deficiency of hydrostatic pressure exists within it, and is transferred to the spindle.   This is seen distinctly near the rudder of a ship in full sail, where the water is much below the level of the surrounding sea.   The cause here, being more evident, and uniform in its nature, may probably be obviated with better success; in as much as this portion of the spindle may not differ essentially from the simple cone.   I fear however, that the whole of this subject is of so dark a nature, as to be more usefully investigated by experiment, than by reasoning; and in the absence of any conclusive evidence from either, the only way that presents itself is to copy nature; accordingly I shall instance the spindles of the trout and woodcock, which, lest the engravings should, in addition to the others, occupy too much valuable space in your Journal, must be reserved to a future opportunity.

A

TREATISE

UPON THE

ART OF FLYING,

BY MECHANICAL MEANS,

WITH A

FULL EXPLANATION OF THE NATURAL PRINCIPLES
BY WHICH BIRDS ARE ENABLED TO FLY;

LIKEWISE

INSTRUCTIONS AND PLANS,

FOR MAKING A FLYING CAR WITH WINGS, IN WHICH A MAN MAY
SIT, AND, BY WORKING A SMALL LEVER, CAUSE HIMSELF TO
ASCEND AND SOAR THROUGH THE AIR WITH THE
FACILITY OF A BIRD.

BY THOMAS WALKER,

PORTRAIT PAINTER, HULL.

HULL:

PRINTED BY JOSEPH SIMMONS, AT THE ROCKINGHAM OFFICE;
AND SOLD BY LONGMAN, HURST, REES, & ORME, LONDON;
AND BY ALL THE PRINCIPAL BOOKSELLERS IN
TOWN AND COUNTRY.

1810.

To the Right Hon. Earl Stanhope.

My Lord, As far as an obscure individual like myself can judge of exalted characters, I am induced, in unison with public opinion, to hold a belief that your lordship is possessed, in a very superior degree, both of genius and a knowledge of the sciences, as well as a known predilection for every thing that is calculated to improve and extend the mechanic arts, or to meliorate the condition of mankind.   To acknowledge also that your lordship is equally preëminent in the senate is but paying a tribute which is *very justly due* to your patriotism, and the great exertions which you have made in advocating the cause of humanity.   Every *friend* to his country must hold in grateful remembrance the energetic and manly opposition which your lordship evinced to prevent the commencement of a war more undefined in its object, more inefficient, and more direful and ruinous in its consequences to our country than any war it was ever madly and unjustly plunged into.   My countrymen have *now* great cause also to remember, with indignation and deep regret, that, in return for your opposition to the origin of those baneful effects, which your lordship clearly foretold, and are now but too severely felt; in return for your wise counsels and patriotic zeal, your lordship met with every coarse insult and contumely which blind folly and malice could suggest.   But your lordship has this inestimable consolation that your life has been most *honourably* engaged not with the savage arts of murder, not with the burning of towns and the destruction of their inoffending and defenceless inhabitants; not with the filling of Europe with miserable widows and orphans; not with the ruin of manufactures and commerce, and the violation of the sacred constitutional rights and liberties of your countrymen; not with the low, base, and contemptible arts of any corrupt and venal faction; not with the arts of tyranny and oppression, or force and fraud; not with the machiavelian arts;

but with the *noble arts* which are conducive to *peace, civiliza-tion*, and the *convenience* and *happiness of mankind*.

Had I invented a diabolical engine that would effectually have swept off from the earth a considerable portion of its *unwary* inhabitants, I should never have thought of addressing your lordship; I must have sought patronage from another quarter; but, considering the subject of this work, I thought no one was more able than your lordship to form a just estima-tion of its merits. I have, therefore, taken the liberty of dedi-cating it to you, flattering myself that the theory it contains will be honoured with your lordship's approbation which will greatly contribute to the pleasure of,

My Lord,
Your Lordship's humble Servant,
THOMAS WALKER.

HULL, February, 1810.

PREFACE.

I AM laying before the public a treatise upon a subject perhaps as extraordinary in its nature as anything that has lately come before them; and after a candid perusal, should it meet with approbation from the friends to arts and sciences, my utmost pride will be gratified. The flight of birds, although so common and familiar to our sight, is certainly as great a phenomenon as any in the creation; and artificial flying, when accomplished, may be considered as one of the greatest wonders of the mechanic arts, which I firmly believe attainable upon the plan I have suggested.

In this little work I have shown that birds' wings do not increase their expansion in exact ratio with the increased specific gravity of their bodies; I have given a demonstration of the cause of the projectile motion of birds, the discovery of a true knowledge of which has bid defiance to philosophers in all ages, which, with other discoveries, I trust will prove that I have given consistency to what henceforth may be denominated the *science* of flying, and which may alone be deemed of considerable importance to science, had nothing more than that been brought forward; but as I have gone much further, and have advanced arguments, and given plans to render the *art of flying practicable*, the importance of this little treatise becomes obvious, more particularly so if we take into consideration the various purposes to which artificial flying may be applied.

When my work was just ready for the press, I was much surprised at the account a friend gave me of what he had seen that day upon flying, in a monthly journal. I immediately procured a sight of it, and found it to be an ingenious paper written by Sir George Cayley, and I own I was astonished at the perusal. I conceived it to be very extraordinary that two persons, not having the least knowledge of each other, should be publishing their thoughts at the same time upon such a subject; nor was I less surprised to find the subject treated of there in a manner so rational and far superior to anything I have ever seen before. From what Sir George has thought, and the calculations he has made upon the subject, he is so sanguine in his belief that flying will be effected as to say, in one part of his paper, as follows: " I feel perfectly confident, however, that this noble art will soon be brought home to man's general convenience, and that we shall be able to transport ourselves and families, and their goods and chattels, more securely by air than by water, and with a velocity of from 20 to 100 miles per hour." — *Vide* Nicholson's Journal for November, 1809.

For my own part, whatever reason I may have to be sanguine of success, I have made a resolution to suppress in my work every thought that confidence could suggest beyond what I could give demonstration of, along with the clearest directions how to attain the end in view; thereby putting it out of the power of critics to say that the principles of my theory have not a good foundation.

Notwithstanding, from the novelty and singularity of the subject, I do expect to meet with a good deal of raillery and sarcasm. The wits will tell me that I am flighty, and the more serious and heavy part of mankind, who are too ponderous for such aerial flights, will express a disapprobation of my scheme; but I do not write for such folks, my sole aim is to deliver my thoughts to the public, in hopes that *men* of *genius* and *science* may turn their attention to a subject that may not before now have attracted their notice, that, by their aid and assistance, the art may be brought into practice; and, as this country stands unrivalled in arts, I hope we shall not be long without a Society for the encouragement of the art of flying. Columbus was laughed at when he talked of a continent beyond the Atlantic; but flighty as he might appear he found it, and *wise* men lost it!

A TREATISE, ETC.

WE learn, from several authors, that, in different ages of the world, the art of flying has been attempted by various means, all of which have hitherto failed of success. When we take into consideration the different methods which are recorded to have been tried, we cannot be surprised that they have all failed, since, compared with what is contained in the following pages, they will obviously appear to be nothing more than mere whims and contrivances, all utterly destitute of the true nature and science of flying.

I am conscious that many of my readers, who have never been led to notice the remarks that many eminently learned men have made upon this art, will be tempted at the first sight of my title page to ridicule a treatise upon artificial flying; for there is not a more common saying, when a person has taken some great difficulty in hand, than that such a thing is as impossible to be done *as for one to fly in the air.* I do assure all such that my treatise is not founded upon a whim of the moment, but from mature deliberation on the display of nature. The study of the works of nature has been to me, during the greatest part of my life, a source of amusement and inexpressible delight. The natural history of birds has particularly occupied my attention, and that enviable faculty which they possess of flying, has greatly excited my curiosity, and led me to that study by which I have obtained *a true knowledge* of the mechanical principles by which they fly, a knowledge which I do not hesitate to declare has hitherto remained undiscovered, although it has been the object of the study and contemplation of many of the most eminent philosophers of past ages.

That great observer of the works of nature, Solomon, did not overlook the subject of flying, but speaks of it in his book of *Proverbs*, xxx, 18, 19 — " There be three things which are too wonderful for me, yea four, which I know not: *the way of an eagle in the air*, the way of a serpent upon a rock." I beg also to remind such of my readers as doubt the possibility of flying that many useful and valuable mechanical inventions, which are now complete and become common, would, a century or two past, have been treated as visionary or impracticable; or had they been accomplished at such periods their effects would have been attributed to witchcraft. I have not the least doubt of being successful in the art of flying, if I had it in my power to give it a fair trial. My invention for attaining the art is founded *entirely upon the principles of nature ;* and although these principles are as old as the creation, they have never, until now, been properly attended to. How much are we indebted to the study of nature for discoveries of the greatest importance? and from this delightful study many more are yet to be expected.

The love of pleasure is natural to man, and to gratify this propensity he eagerly attends to every artificial entertainment that is offered to him. He resorts to theatres and operas, to Newmarket, and other haunts of vanity and folly, as if pleasure were nowhere else to be found; at the same time what an inexhaustible fund of entertainment is overlooked by all but a few, although constantly displayed in the wonderful exhibition of the works of nature.

What a pity it is that minds of men are not more generally and forcibly struck with the pure and tranquil delights resulting from the universal study of nature. What riot, confusion, waste of time, loss of money and of health, might be avoided if this pleasing and truly-enlightening study could be made fashionable. What an infinite stock of ideas it would create; how much it would enrich the human mind, and afford matter for social conversation and entertainment far superior to the unimportant subjects which too generally occupy the minds and tongues of men.

I will now present my readers with some account of various schemes which have been tried to accomplish the art of flying, and shall show the cause of their insufficiency. I shall explain the natural mechanical means by which birds are enabled to fly, and my readers will then be able to judge how far my invention for flying corresponds with the natural science, and is thereby calculated to succeed. I shall show likewise the comparative difference between the specific gravity of the humming bird and the condor, also the different expansion of the wings. I shall compare the weight of a man with the weight of the condor, and thereby determine the necessary dimensions of a pair of wings which would enable a man to fly; and, lastly, I will explain an experiment which I have made, in order to demonstrate the principles of artificial flying, and give directions for making a machine wherein a man may sit, and, by working a pair of wings with a lever, be able to ascend into the air, and fly with as much safety and ease as a bird.

During the early part of my life I have dissected a great many birds, and since studied very minutely the mechanism of their wings, tails, and all the parts which they employ in flying.

I have long been accustomed to contemplate a bird as a living machine, formed by the Almighty Creator, either to run upon the earth, to dive in the waters, or to ascend into or fly through the air; and when I examine its various parts, and find such an exquisite display of wisdom in each being formed so perfectly to answer the use it is applied to; when I see the effect of the whole, that such a wonderfully organized animated piece of matter can quit the earth and soar aloft in the air, it appears to me a miracle, and I am struck with admiration.

It is now almost twenty years since I was first led to think, by the study of birds and their means of flying, that if an artificial machine were formed with wings, in exact imitation of the mechanism of one of those beautiful living machines, and applied in the very same way upon the air, there could be no doubt of its being made to fly; for it is an axiom in philosophy that the same cause will ever produce the same effect.

It is easy to demonstrate that a bird is no more able to fly than a man without the mechanical effect of wing; [1] therefore,

---

[1] The ostrich, in the torrid regions of Africa; the emu, in the extensive plains of Paraguay, in South America, which, standing erect, is about seven feet high, its legs are three

when a man is furnished with a pair of wings large enough, and can apply them in the same manner as a bird does, and with sufficient power, there can be no reason to doubt of a man being able to fly as well as a bird.   The machine which I have planned is as close a copy of the natural mechanism of a bird as artificial means will admit of; and when my readers are made thoroughly acquainted with both the natural and artificial means of flying, I flatter myself they will then be willing to acknowledge that my scheme is a very rational one, highly calculated to insure success in the accomplishment of the art of flying, one of the most extraordinary and desirable arts with which we can be acquainted.

Although I have, for many years, been extremely anxious to bring the machine into effect, and am very sanguine in my expectations of success (for I positively assert that flying cannot be accomplished on any other plan than the one I propose), I, unfortunately, have ever found myself unable, from my professional avocations and other circumstances, to put it in practice, or I should long since have made the experiment.

Finding, therefore, that to no purpose I have deferred, for a long time, its execution, which I deeply regret, and the prospect of the future being not more favourable, I am induced to publish my plan, in the hope that the lovers of the arts and sciences, when I have laid before them a scheme so practicable, will readily be induced, for the honour of science and our country, to contribute to the means of bringing it into practice, and demonstrate to their fellow mortals how they may gain a perfect dominion over another element.

In almost every nation where arts and sciences have flourished, persons have manifested a wish to discover the art of flying.   In Rome and in Paris particularly different persons, and in ages remote from each other, have tried experiments with wings formed of various materials, which have been fastened to their arms, but none of them succeeded, there not

feet long, its thighs are nearly as thick as the thighs of a man, it runs so swift that the fleetest dogs are foiled by it; the cassowary and the dodo, in the Molucca Islands; and the penguins, in the Straits of Magellan and the South Sea Islands.   All these birds are as utterly incapable of flying as a man, none of them being provided with wings for that purpose.

being strength sufficient in a man's arms to enable him to fly with detached wings fastened to him, leaving the whole weight of his body unsupported.

Friar Bacon, who lived nearly five centuries ago, wrote upon the subject, and he affirms that the art of flying is possible; and many others have been of opinion that, by means of artificial wings affixed to the arms or legs, a man might fly as well as a bird.

The philosophers of the reign of King Charles the Second were much engaged with this art. The famous Bishop Wilkin, who, in 1672, published a treatise upon flying, was so confident of its practicability, that he says he does not question but that in future ages it will become as common to hear a man call for wings when going a journey as it is now to call for his boots and spurs.

In the year 1709, as we gather from a letter published in France in 1784, a Portuguese, Friar de Gusman, applied to the king to encourage him in the invention of a flying machine. The principle upon which it was constructed, if indeed it had any principle, seems to have been that of a paper kite. The machine was in the form of a bird, and contained several tubes through which the wind was to pass in order to fill a certain sail, which was to elevate it; and when the wind was deficient the same was to be effected by means of bellows concealed within the body of the machine. The ascent was also to be promoted by the *electric* attraction of pieces of amber placed in the top, and by two *spheres* inclosing *magnets* in the same situation.

These silly inventions show the very low state of science at that time in Portugal, especially as the king, in order to encourage him in his further experiments in such an useful invention, granted him the first vacant place in his College of Barcelos or Santerim, with the first professorship in the University of Coimbra, and an annual pension of 600,000 reis during his life. Of this De Gusman it is also related that, in the year 1736, he made a wicker basket of about seven or eight feet diameter, and covered it with paper, which raised itself about 200 feet in the air, and the effect was generally attributed to witchcraft.

Mr. Willoughby, after observing that the pectoral muscles of a man, in proportion to his weight, are many degrees too weak for flying, recommends to him who would attempt the art with the desire of success to contrive and adapt his wings in such a manner that he may work them with his legs and not with his arms, because the muscles of the legs are much stronger.

The celebrated Lord Bacon wrote on the subject of flying, and believed it practicable, but it seems he could no more direct how it was to be done than any other who had written before him on the same subject.

Thus much, for the satisfaction of my readers, I have thought proper to make mention of what has been attempted in the accomplishment of this wonderful art; but were I to adduce all that has been said and done, at different periods of time, I could compile a large volume of that alone, which would answer no other end than that of curiosity, and to show that no one has ever understood the natural means of flying, which is the only knowledge that can guide us to the completion of artificial flying, and which I hope and trust will be clearly demonstrated in this treatise.

As I shall have occasion to refer to various birds, possessing different powers of flight, in illustration of my design, I here introduce the history of the condor, for the information of such of my readers as may not be acquainted with it.

The condor is a native of America, and hitherto naturalists have been divided whether to refer it to the species of the eagle or to that of the vulture. Its great strength and activity seem to give it a claim to rank among the former, whilst the baldness of its head and neck is thought to degrade it to a rank amongst the latter. It is, however, fully sufficient for our plan to describe its manners, form, weight, expansion, and power; we will therefore leave to nomenclators to decide upon its class. If size (for it is by much the largest bird that flies) and strength, combined with rapidity of flight and rapacity, deserve preëminence, then no bird can be put in competition with it; for the condor possesses, in a higher degree than the eagle, all the qualities that render it formidable not only to the feathered tribe, but to beasts, and even to man himself.

Acosta, Garcilasso, and Desmarchais assert that it measures 18 feet across the wings when expanded; its beak is so strong as to pierce the body of a cow; and it is positively asserted that two of them are capable of devouring that animal. They do not even abstain from attacking man himself; but, fortunately, there are but few of the species. The Indians say that they will carry off a deer or a young calf in their talons as an eagle would a hare or rabbit, that their sight is piercing, and their manners terrific. According to modern authors they only come down to the sea coast at certain seasons, particularly when it is supposed their prey fails them upon the land; that they then feed upon dead fish and such other nutritious substances as the sea throws upon the shore.

Condamine says he has frequently seen them in several parts of the mountains of Quito, and has observed them hovering over a flock of sheep; and he thinks they would, at one particular time, have attempted to carry some of them off had they not been scared away by the shepherds. Labat says that this bird has been described to him, by those who have seen it, as having a body as large as a sheep, and that its flesh is as tough and disagreeable as carrion. The Spaniards residing in that country dread its depredations, there having been *many instances of its carrying off children.* Mr. Strong, the master of a ship, relates that, as he was sailing along the coast of Chili, in the thirty-third degree of South latitude, he observed a bird sitting upon a high cliff near the shore, which one of the ship's company shot with a leaden bullet and killed. They were greatly surprised when they beheld its magnitude, for when the wings were extended they measured 13 feet from one tip to the other; one of the quill feathers was 2 ft. $4\frac{3}{4}$ in. in length, and $1\frac{1}{2}$ in. in circumference.

Mons. Feuilleé, whose description alone is accurate, has given a still more circumstantial account of this amazing bird.

" In a valley of Illo, in Peru," says he, " I discovered a condor perched on a high rock before me. I approached within gun-shot and fired, but as my piece was only charged with swan-shot the lead was not heavy enough to bring the bird down. I perceived, however, by its manner of flying, that it was wounded, and it was with a good deal of difficulty that it flew to another rock about 500 yards distant on the seashore. I therefore charged again with the ball and hit the bird under the throat, which made it mine. I accordingly ran up to seize it; but even in death it was terrible, and defended itself upon its back with its claws extended against me, so that I scarcely knew how to lay hold of it. Had it not been mortally wounded I should have found it no easy matter to take it, but I at last dragged it down from the rock, and, with the assistance of one of the seamen, I carried it to my tent to make a coloured drawing of it. The wings of this bird, which I measured *very exactly*, were 12 ft. 3 in. (English) from tip to tip. The great feathers, which were of a beautiful shining black, were 2 ft. 4 in. long. The thickness of the beak was proportionable to the rest of the body, the length about 4 in., the point hooked downwards and white at its extremity, and the other part was of a black jet. The thigh bones were 10 in. long, the legs 5 in., the toes and claws were in proportion, and the legs were covered with black scales. The little nourishment which these birds find on the coast, except when a tempest throws up some great fish, obliges the condor to continue there but a short time. They usually come to the coast at the approach of evening, stay there all night, and fly back in the morning."

I now proceed to describe the construction and application of the wings of a bird. How properly are they formed to fulfil the uses they were made for! The first is to expand, and by that means to give the bird a secure hold upon the air below it, which hold is always in proportion to the dimensions of the wings. The tail produces the same effect. We see that by means of a pair of wings and a tail duly expanded, in a perfectly *passive state* and aloft in the air, without any muscular motion, a bird procures a suspending power, which counteracts the specific gravity of its body, and prevents it being precipitated to the ground; such is the effect of the wings and tail when in a *passive state*.

I will next take some notice of the quill feathers, which are replete with proofs of the wisdom of the Almighty artist who made them. As they were intended to swim within so light and subtle a fluid as the air is, it was necessary that they should be formed of the lightest materials imaginable; and as they were intended to strike upon the air with great power and rapidity, it was requisite that they should possess in the shafts great strength with elasticity; it was expedient too that the quill feathers should separate and open to let the upper air pass through the wings, to facilitate their ascent when they are struck upwards; it was also necessary that they should all shut close together, forming each wing into a complete surface or web, when they are, by the muscular power of the bird, forced down in order to give a more secure hold upon the air below, and by that means keep the bird up.

Now if we do but examine the quill feathers we shall find in the shafts astonishing strength with elasticity, and very little specific gravity indeed. The webs of the quill feathers are broader on one side of the shaft than the other, which causes them to open as the wings move up and to shut as they come down, exactly answering the purposes I have already mentioned; therefore, we see how wonderfully-complete the wings are in all their parts, and how effectually they serve all the uses required.

I will now show the application and effect of the wings and tail in *an active* state. When a bird, by the power of its pectoral and deltoid muscles, puts its wings into action and strikes them downwards in a perfectly vertical direction upon the air below, that air being compressed by the stroke of the wings makes a resistance, by its elastic power, against the under side of the wings, in proportion to the rapidity of the stroke and the dimensions of the wings, and forces the bird upwards; at the same time the back edges of the wing being more weak or elastic than the fore-edges, they give way to the resisting power of the compressed air, which rushes upwards *past the same back edges*, acting against them with its elastic power, and thereby *causes a projectile force*, which impels the bird forwards; thus we see that by one act of the wings the bird produces both *buoyancy* and *progression*. When the tail is forced upwards, and the wings are in action, the bird ascends and forced downwards it consequently descends; but the most *important use of the tail is to support the posterior weight of the bird*, and to prevent the vacillation of the whole.

Thus having discovered and explained to my readers the natural machanical means by which birds accomplish flying, they will be able to see that the plan upon which I have formed my scheme for artificial flying is perfectly analogous to the principles of nature, which certainly ought to be clearly understood, and taken as our only guide, before we can ever expect to arrive at success in the art of flying; but with the knowledge of these principles *there cannot remain a doubt of success.*

When we first think of a man attempting to fly by mechanical means, we are induced, considering his specific gravity to pronounce it impossible; and had we never seen or known of any bird larger than a humming bird, whose weight does not exceed one drachm, and whose diminutive wings measure only three inches from tip to tip; and were to be told by some traveller that he had seen a bird with a body as large as a sheep, that had wings of twelve feet expansion, and that it could quit the earth and ascend into the air with its ponderous body, and there fly about with as much ease as the little humming bird, we should think it too marvellous a tale to be credited. But as we are accustomed to see, almost every day, birds of such various dimensions and specific gravity as are exhibited by nature, from the humming bird to the common wren; from the wren, through a numerous gradation, up to the eagle, we can readily give credit to the history of the wonderful condor in South America, whose existence is so well attested that we can have no reason to doubt of it, more especially as we witness so vast a gradation in the indigenous birds of our own country. I believe that there were two of these prodigious birds in the Leverian Museum.

The following observations upon the wonderful difference in the weight of some birds, with their apparent means of supporting it in their flight, may tend to remove some prejudices against my plan from the minds of some of my readers. The weight of the humming bird is one drachm, that of the condor not less than four stone. Now, if we reduce four stone into drachms, we shall find the condor is 14,336 times as heavy as the humming bird. What an amazing disproportion of weight! Yet by the same mechanical use of its wings, the condor can overcome the specific gravity of its body with as much ease as the little humming bird. But this is not all. We are informed that this enormous bird possesses a power in its wings, so far exceeding what is necessary for its own conveyance through the air, that it can take up and fly away with a whole sheep in its talons, with as much ease as an eagle would carry off, in the same manner, a hare or a rabbit. This we may readily give credit to, from the known fact of our little kestril and the sparrow hawk frequently flying off with a partridge, which is nearly three times the weight of these rapacious little birds.

Let us attend to this subject a little further. Let us consider these wings of the condor, which, with a *mechanical action alone*, produces a power that is capable of carrying through the air both the bird and the sheep, weighing together not less than ten stone, which would then be 204,000 *times the weight of the humming bird !* When this is duly considered, with reference to my plan, what encouragement does it not give to prosecute the art of flying? particularly so when we consider that a man of ten stone weight, in a machine weighing two stone, will only exceed the weight of the condor *one-fifth part ;* this is a mere trifle compared with the astonishing difference there is between the humming bird and the condor.

The condor carries ten stone, with wings of twelve feet expansion from tip to tip; the humming bird carries one drachm, with three inches expansion; the common wren is three times as heavy as the humming bird, and has but one inch more of wing; a pigeon weighs 16 ounces, which is 256 times as heavy as it is, and has only ten times more expansion of wing; the goatsucker is forty times as heavy, and has seven times the length of wing. I could here carry the same observations upon other birds to a very great extent, but the above are instances sufficient to prove that birds' wings are not multiplied in their length in the same proportion with the increased weight of their bodies: therefore, as a man weighing ten stone and his machine two, as I have already shown, will only exceed in weight *one-fifth part* of the weight of the condor and his prey; and as the wings of the condor are about twelve feet, suppose we make a pair of wings of silk, one-fifth longer than they are, which will be about fourteen feet and a half, I am thoroughly persuaded they will be found amply sufficient, as they will far exceed the progressive increase of birds' wings.

By attending to the progressive increase of the weight of birds, from the delicate little humming bird up to the huge condor, we clearly discover that the addition of a few ounces, pounds, or stones, is no obstacle to the art of flying; the specific weight of birds *avails nothing*, for by their *possessing wings large enough*, and *sufficient power to work them*, they can accomplish the means of flying equally well upon all the various scales and dimensions which we see in nature.

Such being *a fact*, in the name of reason and philosophy why shall not a man with a pair of artificial wings, *large enough* and with *sufficient power to strike them upon the air*, be able to produce the same effect.

I shall, after a few observations, proceed to describe how a machine may be made with a pair of wings, and a lever to work them with, so that any person will be able to see how far it is calculated to answer the purpose for which it is intended. This machine may be considered as a large artificial bird, and the man placed in the inside as the vital or moving power. All the attempts hitherto made in the art of flying, by different persons, according to historians, have been mere childish whims, not in the least degree calculated to insure success. They each made a pair of detached wings, some of silk, some of leather, and some of sheet iron and various other materials; they fastened them upon their shoulders or arms: thus equipped, they placed themselves upon some eminence, such as a high tower or a church steeple, then took to their wings; but few of them were fortunate enough to escape without some injury.

It is utterly impossible for a man to fly with a pair of wings fixed to his shoulders or arms, with the whole weight of his body hanging down and depending entirely on his pectoral muscles for support. These muscles in a man are many degrees too weak to keep extended a pair of wings of sufficient expansion to effectually counteract the specific gravity of his body. Let a man suspend the weight of his body, with his arms extended, holding to an horizontal beam by his hands and he will very soon find the insufficiency of the strength of his arms to support his weight. On the plan which I have conceived for flying the want of strength in the arms is amply provided for. By furnishing a man with a car to sit in, the whole weight of his body is supported by it, and as he sits much in the same manner as if he were rowing a boat, he is enabled to bring into action his *whole bodily strength, which far exceeds* the strength of his arms only, and by sitting in such a position his strength can be exerted with a far greater force than in any other attitude whatever; he at the same time gains an *additional advantage*, in this plan of mine by exerting his strength upon a lever.

The two greatest requisites for accomplishing the art of flying are these — first, *expansion of wings large enough* to resist, in a sufficient degree, the specific gravity of whatever is attached to them; second, *strength enough* to strike the wings with a sufficient force to complete the buoyancy, and give a projectile motion to the machine. With these two requisites combined *flying must be accomplished;* and, upon my plan there can be no doubt of wings being made as large as ever they may be wanted; neither ought we to doubt of a man's ability, exerting himself in the way I have described to bring into action as great a degree of strength, in proportion to his weight, as the condor is possessed of. Therefore, if we are secure of these two requisites, and I am very confident we are, we may calculate upon the success of flying with as much certainty as upon our walking.

When I first thought of artificial flying, it occurred to me that it would be of some importance to try what effect a pair of wings would have upon the air, without any mechanical power to work them; I thought that if I were to suspend a weight from beneath them, and they should prevent that weight from falling in a perpendicular line to the ground, they would demonstrate that the ideas I had conceived of the cause of the projectile motion of birds were well founded.

I therefore made the following experiment, to which I call the *particular attention of my readers, as it positively demonstrates the cause of the projectile motion.* I made a pair of small wings, of fine paper, and very small slips of wood to keep them extended, and fixed on a tail of the same materials, imitating, as near as I could, the wings and tail of a bird when expanded in a *passive state.* I then suspended a small weight from under them, with a piece of thread, exactly in the centre of gravity; I held them up as high as I could reach, then took away my hand and left them flat upon the air, without giving any impulse to them whatever; and by the weight pressing downwards the air under the wings became, in some degree, compressed, and by its reaction against the under side and the back edges of the wings, *they were projected with an oblique descent from one end of the room to the other, carrying the weight all that distance,* which, without the wings being of this particular construction, could not have been done.

I had cause sufficient to exult in the success of my experiment, which proved to me, in a very satisfactory manner, that what I had conceived to be the cause of the projectile motion of birds *was really the cause,* and that if I could but give a vertical motion to the wings, so that they might strike upon the air with a sufficient force, they would then increase the reaction of the air, and instead of being projected in an oblique descent, totally overcome their specific gravity, and *continue flying in an horizontal direction.*

This is an experiment which any of my readers may make trial of for their own satisfaction and amusement.

Another experiment, serving to shew the different effect of buoyancy obtained by a parachute and by my paper wings may be tried in the following manner: — Take two straight sticks, neatly dressed, about the thickness of a crow-quill and each about sixteen inches long, lay them across each other in the middle, at right angles, and tie them fast with a piece of thread; then tie a piece of thread from the ends of one stick to the other, so as to secure them at right angle: then take a sheet of gauze paper, and fasten all the four corners of it to the four ends of the sticks; but previous to this, paste upon the four corners of the paper four small slips of thin cloth in order to give sufficient strength; then suspend any small weight by a thread from the centre; let the whole fall from a height, and you will see the effect of a parachute in miniature: but this effect is very different from that of the paper wings; the parachute *sinks gradually down in a perpendicular line*, whilst the wings *dart forwards* to the distance of several yards.

I have met with persons who have boldly asserted that it is impossible for a man to exert sufficient strength to raise himself up into the air by mechanical means alone; but the rashness and fallacy of such an assertion is completely refuted and exposed by Mr. Degen, in Vienna, who has very lately actually ascended *into the air*, to a considerable height, by sitting in a machine and giving action to two parachutes; and had he properly understood the principles of birds' wings, and considered the astonishing power in the reaction of the air, which may be *increased in proportion to any force* exerted upon it, *ad infinitum*, and possessed a complete knowledge of the principles upon which it enables birds to fly, he would have chose wings and not parachutes, and might then have accomplished flying in perfection.[1]

There is no doubt that, by large parachutes, worked by a mechanical power, a man may raise himself from the ground to a considerable height; but that cannot be properly called flying, because as the compressed air rushes from underneath the parachutes, to regain its equilibrium *on all sides alike*, there

---

[1] M. Degen, a watchmaker of Vienna, has invented a machine by which a person may raise himself into the air. It is formed of two parachutes, of taffeta, which may be folded up or extended at pleasure, and the person who moves them is placed in the centre. M. Degen has made several public experiments, and rose to the height of fifty-four feet, flying, in various directions, with the celerity of a bird. A subscription has been opened at Vienna to enable the inventor to prosecute his discoveries. — *Vide* the Monthly Magazine for September, 1809.

can be no *projectile motion* effected, without which *there can be no command or steerage*, and in such case the whole apparatus will be driven which ever way the wind impels it; I therefore cannot give credit to that part of the account of M. Degen's performance which asserts that he flew *in various directions*, although I can readily believe in his having raised himself into the air, and think that great praise is due to him. I do not believe it possible, upon his plan, that he could have gone in any other direction than with the wind; but with a pair of wings constructed and worked according to the natural principles of flying, a projectile motion is obtained in as perfect a manner as buoyancy, *both of which* must be accomplished before we can have the benefit and pleasure of flying with steerage, and that upon the following plan only, viz. :—

Make a car of as light materials as possible, but with sufficient strength to support a man in it; provide a pair of wings of about eight feet each in length, let them be horizontally expanded, and fastened upon the top edge on each side of the car, with two joints each, so as to admit of a vertical motion to the wings, which motion may be effected by a man sitting and working an upright lever in the middle of the car; a tail of about seven or eight feet long, and the same breadth at its extremity, must be fixed to the hinder part of the car, and spread out flat to the horizon in the same manner as we see the tails of birds.

The grebes, by their manner of flying, evince that the most important use of a bird's tail is *to support* the *posterior weight* of the body; for the Creator having left the whole of this class of birds, of which we have five different species indigenous in this country, all totally destitute of any portion of a tail, they are, consequently, always seen when flying to have their bodies hanging down nearly in a perpendicular direction, and appear to fly with great difficulty; but this impediment in flying is of little consequence to them, their organization being perfectly adapted to their mode of living. They find their subsistence in lakes and pools, wherein they are incessantly diving, and, of course, are not obliged to fly until those places are frozen up, when they are compelled to flutter off, as well as they are able, in search of some spring or swamp which is not affected by frost, where they find a temporary subsistence until their favourite lakes are relieved from a surface of ice; they then return to their former haunts, when they again seem quite in their element. Here we find a class of birds, owing to their want of tails, possessing the power of flight in a very imperfect degree, compared with some birds. It also may be observed that birds having extraordinary large tails, as the magpie for instance, do not fly in the best manner; none of these birds possess what seems to constitute the excellence of flying, viz., soaring and reposing upon the air; this can only be effected when the weight of the body is upon an equipoise in the centre of the wings and tail, each bearing up its due proportion, and the expansion altogether so large, as to bring the whole weight nearly in equilibrium with the atmosphere. This must be properly attended to in the construction of a flying machine.

To give a further security to the power of suspension, a sail of an equilateral triangle may be spread horizontally over the man's head, supported by a small light mast or bowsprit, at the height of three or four feet above the car; the sail must be expanded and fixed to the mast by a very light yard, presenting the base of the sail to the head of the car, with the opposite point towards the tail, and there fastened with a cord to another small bowsprit; this sail will be a protection, if large enough, in case of any accident occurring to the machine; it will then prevent the man from being precipitated to the ground in a manner similar to a parachute. I only have mentioned this sail that it may be resorted to if it be found necessary in a long voyage; the first experiment I would try without it.

A coachmaker is accustomed to make strong work with little weight of materials; he, therefore, would be the most proper person to make a machine of this kind. The man must sit in the middle, between the wings and the tail, so as to be a little behind the centre of gravity, for the purpose of causing a little preponderance of weight to act upon the back edge of the wings; for if there be not, in some degree, more weight behind than before, when the compressed air is making a resistance against the underside and back edges of the wings, where it rushes upwards again, causing a great reaction, it would, of course, elevate the hinder part of the car too much.

The wings and the tail should be made of silk, very compactly woven, and as impervious to the air as possible. The silk which the wings are formed of, should be laid on in separate broad slips,[1] and should open to admit the air to pass through as the wings move up, and close together again as they come down, in the same manner as I have described the action of the quill feathers in the wings of birds; although, upon the experiment being tried, this method may not be found so absolutely requisite, for we see flying squirrels, bats, butterflies, beetles, flying fish, etc., with wings formed of compact membranes, all flying exceedingly well. The Madagascar bat has a body the size of a rabbit, with wings four feet long, formed of entire membranes, and, although so large, it can fly as well as our little native bats; therefore it is possible that a pair of artificial wings may be formed without any valves, and yet answer equally well; but this can only be determined by actual trial.

It is necessary to observe that the car in which the man is to sit must be entirely covered on the outside with silk or very thin leather, and along each side of the car the silk or leather must be united to the base of the wings, to prevent as much as possible, the air from escaping anywhere but from the back edges of the wings: should that be neglected, when the air is compressed by the wings being struck downwards, it will rush upwards through the car and thereby fail of giving that resistance against the underside of the wings which is necessary for the purpose of effecting buoyancy and progression.

I think that the shafts of the wings and tail would answer the purpose in the best manner, if they were each of them made of six long slips of thin whalebone, dressed tapering to a point, then wrapped together in a round form with small twine from end to end, and filled with cork along the inside. By making

---

[1] The tail feathers of turkies laid close and parallel to each other and fast sewed upon eight pieces of strong riband, so as to form the same number of slips, then extended in the wing and well braced, would perhaps answer the purpose much better.

them in this manner they would spring against the air, would
be very light, and so strong that it would be impossible to
break them with the power or weight of any one person. By
forming them as above we shall humbly imitate the shaft of a
quill feather, which is composed of a thin horny shell, containing a delicate light pith along the inside.

I here recommend my readers to *particularly observe* that a
main point in this treatise is that they should not overlook the
importance of the knowledge of the reaction of the air against
the underside and *back edges of the wings*, for this is what
causes the projectile motion, which is indisputably proved by
the flying of my paper wings across a room, and which I will
further illustrate by the flight of birds, mill sails, &c.

I have frequently conversed with persons about the art of flying by mechanical means, and generally found them disposed
to treat the idea with ridicule. I have asked them if they knew
how birds were enabled to fly, and they mostly answered me
nearly in the following manner: that birds could fly because it
was natural to them, that they were covered with feathers, which
were such light materials as to help them to fly, and that their
wings are properly adapted for flying. This was as far as they
could explain, which proved that *all* they knew on this subject
amounted to nothing. They generally seemed to indulge an
idea that there was something in the flight of birds either super-
natural or incomprehensible; but I hope my readers will be
convinced, by this little treatise, that the art of flying is as truly
mechanical as the art of rowing a boat.

I will here further illustrate how flying is effected. The air,
when struck upon by wings, produces an effect by its reaction
against the underside and back edges, similar to that which is
caused by the wind blowing with sufficient force against a mill-
sail, when it *rushes off on one side*, and impels the sail to move,
with this difference only, that the sail, being fastened at one end
to an axis, is made to revolve, whilst the bird, being at full
liberty in the air, is caused, by the expansive power of the air
acting with a resisting force *against the back edges* of the wings,
to glide forward in a right line.

Most of my readers, I think, will acknowledge the great elastic power of the wind, as it is manifested by the sailing of ships and the revolving of mill-sails; these effects are produced by the wind being compressed against the sails from its own natural motion and force; but the effect the air has against the wings or sails of birds is produced by its being compressed, with them striking vertically upon it; and the larger they are made the greater quantity of air is compressed, by which means is caused a more powerful reaction, and consequently a more effectual buoyancy and progression. From this cause all the birds whose wings are *very large* in proportion to their weight are able to fly with the *least exertion* imaginable, whilst birds with very small wings are obliged to use very great labour indeed; this being demonstrated by the examination of the dimensions of birds' wings and their specific gravity, and by observing their different methods of flying.

I have often been delighted with the striking conviction that Supreme wisdom alone could have so nicely adjusted all the various internal and external organization of the vast number of different species of birds, to their diversified wants and modes of living; but it is only necessary to observe here that all those which are under the greatest necessity of flying are provided with the *longest* and *best proportion* of *wings* and *tails*, and are consequently able to fly in the best manner, and those which need them less have them more limited, and are therefore less capable of flying, as if the all-wise Creator had set limits to their powers of flight, that they might not go out of their respective elements.

Although I think that a pair of wings seven or eight feet each in length would be sufficient, still, if I could make it convenient to try the experiment of flying, and were not prevented, as I am, by a chain of untoward and uncontrollable circumstances, I would cause the wings to be made of as large dimensions as I could possibly *move with ease.*

I observe amongst the aquatic birds that the auks, guillemots, divers, etc., have such remarkably small narrow wings that they would be utterly incapable of keeping themselves up in the air if it were not for an exertion which they are obliged to make in the extreme. Their wings are moved with such rapidity as to be with difficulty discerned. In this we see the economy of the all-wise Creator, for according to their habits and appetites they have very little occasion to fly at any time, except during the time of incubation, when they have to ascend the most inaccessible rocks and cliffs they meet with along the sea shore, where they breed and rear their young; all the rest of their time they pass on or in the water, swimming and diving for their food.

All the gallinaceous class of birds have very short concave wings, which they strike with great exertion; they also, in general, have but little occasion to fly; their food, which con sists principally of grain and seeds, being spontaneously scattered over the earth, they are almost constantly upon their legs, running about to pick it up, and seldom fly but to avoid danger.

On the other hand, rapacious birds, whose appetites induce them to be the greatest part of their time upon the wing, in search of a subsistence which is very precarious (as every inferior bird, &c., to which they direct their sanguinary attacks, from that love of existence which God has so strongly implanted in all His creatures, will use its utmost skill and activity to elude its destroyer), are much better accommodated, having wings of large dimensions they can repose upon the air, and project themselves forward with a gentle wafting. This is the class of birds I would copy from in the construction of a machine for artificial flying. The kite or glead, P, B, Z, (or *milvus* from Lin.,) is the best natural specimen that we can find in the British ornithology; this bird has very large flat wings, with a large forked tail, and flies with the least exertion, I believe, of any bird in the creation.

All the hyrundo class of birds are almost constantly flying; they all have bodies of little weight, have large *flat* wings, and fly with great ease. The goat-sucker, which is a species of nocturnal swallow, is admirably constructed for flying with facility.

As I have mentioned aquatic birds, I will here take the

opportunity of execrating, with all the indignation of my soul, that savage and brutal amusement which they bring to my mind, and which so many persons frequently practice and take delight in; I mean the shooting these harmless and inoffensive birds. Many are the parties who resort to Flamborough-head, for no other purpose than gratifying their vanity by making a display of their dexterity in shooting, and causing all the havock they possibly can amongst the poor inoffensive birds. Barren must be their minds, and callous their feelings, who can take pleasure in destroying these innocent creatures, which are not in the smallest degree offensive to man when they are living, nor of the least service to him when killed. If these *gentlemen* could eat them when they have done shooting, that would be some excuse; but as their flesh is very rancid these wanton barbarians have no relish for their game. I wish their humanity was as nice as their appetites, they would not find delight in merely shooting them for sport and cruelty, leaving them, some killed and others wounded, floating on the surface of the sea, whilst their helpless young ones must consequently perish with hunger upon the shelvings of the rocks. Such amusements, surely, are not becoming rational beings, but may give pleasure to semi-rationals.

In the months of May and June these birds, which, during the rest of their time are dispersed over various parts of the ocean, are brought by one of the great impulses of nature to assemble at Flamborough-head in myriads, producing a throng, upon a great extent of cliff, similar to what we see in miniature in the front of a bee-hive, on a fine summer's day, when there is a perpetual egress and ingress of thousands.

A person who has never seen such a sight, and is capable of deriving pleasure from contemplating the economy and the works of nature, may find an exquisite gratification in paying a visit, at this season of the year, to Flamborough-head without having recourse to wanton acts of cruelty. Will there ever come upon the earth a generation of men who will despise all pleasures that are either unreasonable or inhuman?

Reason and *humanity* constitute the *only* permanent basis of all human happiness, and *real* honour and true glory of man! without which he is but a compound of folly and madness, and is too often a vile mischievous brute.   By a disregard and contempt of these two divine guides families and nations become distracted and are made miserable, as we have too amply witnessed in the deplorable and wretched state in which Europe has been so long afflicted, where the appetite of the cannibal has *only* been wanting to complete the brutality of *civilized* nations.   But I am departing too much from my original subject; I will withdraw my pen from this sickening view of poor, frail, erring, human nature!

After having described how to construct a machine to fly in, which, like the swift or great black martin (*apus*, Lin.), cannot fly from the surface of the ground, but must have an elevation to rise from, it becomes necessary that I should give directions how it may be made to ascend.   Set two tressels fast upon the ground, one six feet high and the other four and a half, at twelve feet distance from each other; then lay upon them two or three planks, which will form a stage with an oblique plane, upon which the car must be placed, with its head pointing to the higher end of the stage.

A person may then get into the car, and sit a little behind the centre of gravity, which must be adjusted before the car is placed there; being thus elevated he will have depth enough on each side of the car to admit of his wings striking upon the air. He must then push the lever forward about eighteen inches from its perpendicular line, the tips of the wings will then rise three feet and a half above the level of their joints; he must then, with a brisk exertion, pull the lever backwards eighteen inches past the perpendicular line, and the tips of the wings will be struck downwards, passing through an arch of seven feet and suddenly driving down and compressing the air in that arch, part of which will escape past the back edge of the wings (as I have described before), making at the same time a reaction which will push the wings forward: and as the car and the wings are first placed on an oblique plane, they will be impelled forwards, making an oblique ascent.   The projectile impulse will naturally force the machine upwards in an angle in which the plane of the wings is laid, somewhat similar to what may be observed in the raising of a common paper kite, except in a right angle, or perpendicular line; but the nearer the angle of ascent inclines to the line of the horizon, the easier will the machine be found to ascend. I believe pigeons can ascend very near in a perpendicular line, but such an ascent would be too incommodious for artificial flying.

When the car is brought to a sufficient altitude to clear the tops of hills, trees, buildings, &c., the man, by sitting a little forward on his seat, will then bring the wings upon an horizontal plane, and by continuing the action of the wings he will be impelled forwards in that direction. To descend, he must desist from striking the wings, and hold them on a level with their joints; the car will then gradually come down, and when it is within five or six feet of the ground, the man must instantly strike the wings downwards, and *sit as far back* as he can; he will by this means check the projectile force, and cause the car to alight very gently with a retrograde motion. The car, when up in the air, may be made to turn to the right or the left, merely by the man inclining the weight of his body to one side.

When I have seen a man sitting in a chair upon a tight rope, with a table before him, spread over with decanters, glasses, &c., &c., and, by his *dexterity alone*, be able to keep himself and all his accommodations exactly balanced there while he sat smoking his pipe, apparently at perfect ease; I have been induced to consider the art of managing a flying machine, compared with such a surprizing display of human dexterity, to be very simple; and see no reason why men should not become as expert in navigating the air as the sea.

As some of my readers, who may have little regard for anything but the *utile*, may be induced to ask, what use will flying be of, when it is attained? I beg leave, in the way of reply, to give the following hints: — I hope it will be granted that flying will be of great use, if by such means we can have our letters, newspapers, &c., conveyed to any part of the kingdom at the rate of forty or fifty miles in an hour, or if that numerous class of mercantile agents who are now denominated riders, henceforth be enabled to glide through the air with great expedition, in flying machines; or if a man, by such means, can take a rope to any mariners in distress along the sea coast, and thereby become the happy instrument of saving their lives; and if the circumnavigator be able to quit his ship, fly and explore the interior parts of a new discovered island, free from the annoyance and hostilities of its rude inhabitants — but it would be tedious to enumerate all the uses to which artificial flying may be applied: it is obvious enough that when one man is enabled to fly, thousands may do the same, either on business or pleasure. It may tend greatly to reduce the vast number of horses kept in this kingdom, and by that means a very great quantity of land which is taken up at present in growing hay, oats, and beans for the support of these quadrupeds, might be then cultivated for the increase of our national stock of subsistence for the population: and I think it is evident that we have great occasion to reduce the superfluous number of those animals, and to employ all the land we possibly can to grow corn, &c., for our own subsistence. It is not improbable, that some persons will ask, if flying and all this can be accomplished: to which I answer, that if my scheme for attaining the art be deemed a rational one, as I hope it will, I think we certainly ought to try the experiment.

After the perusal of this work, I hope my readers will be fully convinced, that all attempts which have been hitherto made in the art of flying have failed, not in consequence of the art being impracticable, but from the natural science of flying having never yet been fully understood. All that has ever been written, and all the experiments that have ever been made towards attaining a knowledge of artificial flying by mechanical means, display a chaos of unsettled thoughts very wide and deficient of the principles of nature; but I hope it will be granted that I have clearly discovered and demonstrated the whole of those principles upon which flying depends,

particularly the *cause* of the *projectile motion* of birds. This
is a discovery of the greatest importance, for as the air is
continually acting, in the manner I have described, against the
back edges of the wings, and thereby impelling the bird
forwards with great force, *it positively has as much tendency to
overcome specific gravity as the expansion of the wings has.*
This is a fact demonstrated very clearly by my paper wings
and by the manner of flying peculiar to some birds, particularly the woodpeckers. When one of these extraordinary birds
has struck its wings once or twice upon the air, and thereby
produced a projectile impulse sufficient to force it forward
to a considerable distance, it instantly contracts its wings as
close to *its sides* as when perched on a bough, and continues
flying several yards with its wings kept *close* in that position,
until the impulse is abating; it then throws out its wings again,
gives another stroke or two to renew the impulse, shuts them
up and is again driven forward; thus continuing to fly by distinct and separate projectile impulses alone. Here then we see
the great importance of a true knowledge of the cause of
the projectile motion of birds, for this surprising bird does not
depend upon a continued expansion of wings to keep itself
up in the air, but is kept up and carried forward by the projectile force alone!

The green woodpecker is about the size of a pigeon, and,
as it is very common in every part of England where wood
abounds, many of my readers may have an opportunity of
observing its curious method of flying; the same may be observed of the beautiful little goldfinch, and of linnets. Here
the physico-theologist, who is accustomed to contemplate the
wisdom of God in all His works, might be led to infer that He
has caused this deviation from the general method of flying, in
order to demonstrate to us the *effect* of the projectile *force*, and
that it is one of the *greatest essentials* in the art of flying, and
perfectly distinct from and independent of the continued expansion of wings.

When we see pigeons flying *upwards* in the angle of *sixty* or
seventy, as we do every day, from the streets to the tops of

houses, with the plane of their wings parallel to the line of their ascent, I think they prove in a satisfactory manner the great effect of the *projectile force;* for without we admit this to be the cause of their ascending in such angles, how can we possibly account for it in any other way, upon rational principles?

A stone thrown by the hand, and a ball ejected from the mouth of a cannon, are made to overcome specific gravity, and fly to a great distance; we all know that these are not kept up by wings, but entirely by the projectile force. In fact, it is by the air being made continually to push the bird forwards, which constitutes the main cause of flying.

We must attribute to a total ignorance of the fundamental principles, that the art of flying has not been brought hitherto into common practice; for an art, so practicable as it is, must at any period of time have soon succeeded a discovery, such as I have made; and now that the art appears so very attainable, I hope that every friend to arts and sciences will acknowledge that it ought to have a fair trial.

I shall now conclude my treatise on flying with an appeal to the candour and good sense of my readers, whether the arguments I have used, and the principles upon which I have insisted the art of flying may be accomplished, are not such as give it a just claim to their approbation; for I think I may affirm, without being accused of arrogance, that the art of flying has never before been treated of upon such rational and scientific principles.[1]

---

[1] I will here take the liberty of communicating a few hints, which I conceive to be of importance to the aërostatic science. Now that we know the true cause of the projectile motion of birds, and I having suggested a plan for producing the same effect by artificial means, we may be able to accomplish what Messrs. Roberts, Blanchard, and others attempted to do, but in vain, entirely from their not possessing a knowledge of this mystery of nature. I am alluding to the steerage of balloons, which they endeavoured, with great labour, to attain, by striking a number of oars *horizontally* against the air; and if we do but take into consideration that the balloon was constantly flying from the air against which they were striking, it does not seem probable that they could, by such means, produce the effect they aimed at.

But if we make a car from the plan which I have laid down in this treatise, and upon a scale large enough to admit of one of Messrs. Mead and Co.'s new invented revolving steam engines, to move the lever with, we then can work, in a *vertical direction*, a pair of

Having now submitted to the good sense of my countrymen the whole of what I intended on the subject of flying, I, for the present, most respectfully take my leave of them, indulging a hope that the prediction of Bishop Wilkins, expressed in a former page, will soon be verified, and trusting that I shall not be disappointed in the opinion I entertain respecting the patronage which they will extend towards the invention now laid before them. Encouraged by the public, I shall not abandon my purpose of making still further exertions to advance and complete an art, the discovery of the *true principles* of which, I trust, I can with verity affirm to be exclusively my own.

---

very large wings, which would produce a *projectile force* sufficient to impel the balloon forwards in any point of the compass to which we might incline it; and by having a large tail fixed to the car, in an universal joint, we should be able to give it any inclination whatever; and when we have thus effected a perfect steerage to balloons, we shall be able to convey a number of passengers to any place of destination with accuracy and safety. But for this kind of navigation the balloon must be much smaller than usual, and perfectly spherical, and the gas should be kept in such a degree as not to have too great a tendency to ascend — it should be so regulated as to float in equilibrium with the atmosphere; the aëronauts could then keep the machine at a moderate height — from fifty to a hundred feet would be high enough for ordinary sailing, and if it was found to be inclining too much upwards, it might be counteracted by holding the tail in a descending direction. One of Mr. Mead's patent steam engines can be made with a one-horse power, or equal to the strength of eight or ten men, that will not weigh more than eight stone; and will stand in the small space of four feet by two, with the boiler and all the apparatus belonging to it.

WENHAM ON AERIAL LOCOMOTION.

THE following paper, "On Aerial Locomotion and the Laws by which Heavy Bodies impelled through Air are Sustained," was read by F. H. Wenham, Esq., at the first meeting of the Aeronautical Society of Great Britain, held on the 27th day of June, 1866. His Grace the Duke of Argyll in the Chair.

The resistance against a surface of a defined area, passing rapidly through yielding media, may be divided into two opposing forces. One arising from the cohesion of the separated particles; and the other from their weight and inertia, which, according to well-known laws, will require a constant power to set them in motion.

In plastic substances, the first condition, that of cohesion, will give rise to the greatest resistance. In water this has very little retarding effect, but in air, from its extreme fluidity, the cohesive force becomes inappreciable, and all resistances are caused by its weight alone; therefore, a weight, suspended from a plane surface, descending perpendicularly in air, is limited in its rate of fall by the weight of air that can be set in motion in a given time.

If a weight of 150 lbs. is suspended from a surface of the same number of square feet, the uniform descent will be 1,300 feet per minute, and the force given out and expended on the air, at this rate of fall, will be nearly six horse-power; and, conversely, this same speed and power must be communicated to the surface to keep the weight sustained at a fixed altitude. As the surface is increased, so does the rate of descent and its accompanying power, expended in a given time, decrease. It might, therefore, be inferred that, with a sufficient extent of surface reproduced, or worked up to a higher altitude, a man might by his exertions raise himself for a time, while the surface descends at a less speed.

A man, in raising his own body, can perform 4,250 units of work — that is, this number of pounds raised one foot high per minute — and can raise his own weight — say, 150 lbs. — twenty-two feet per minute. But at this speed the atmospheric resistance is so small that 120,000 square feet would be required to balance his exertions, making no allowance for weight beyond his own body.

We have thus reasons for the failure of the many misdirected attempts that have, from time to time, been made to raise weights perpendicularly in the air by wings or descending surfaces. Though the flight of a bird is maintained by a constant reaction or abutment against an enormous weight of air in comparison with the weight of its own body, yet, as will be subsequently shown, the support upon that weight is not necessarily commanded by great extent of wing-surface, but by the direction of motion.

One of the first birds in the scale of flying magnitude is the pelican. It is seen in the streams and estuaries of warm climates, fish being its only food. On the Nile, after the inundation, it arrives in flocks of many hundreds together, having migrated from long distances. A specimen shot was found to weigh twenty-one pounds, and measured ten feet across the wings, from end to end. The pelican rises with much difficulty, but, once on the wing, appears to fly with very little exertion, notwithstanding its great weight. Their mode of progress is peculiar and graceful. They fly after a leader, in one single train. As he rises or descends, so his followers do the same in succession, imitating his movements precisely. At a distance, this gives them the appearance of a long undulating ribbon, glistening under the cloudless sun of an oriental sky. During their flight they make about seventy strokes per minute with their wings. This uncouth-looking bird is somewhat whimsical in its habits. Groups of them may be seen far above the earth, at a distance from the river-side, *soaring*, apparently for their own pleasure. With outstretched and motionless wings, they float serenely, high in the atmosphere, for more than an hour together, traversing the same locality in circling movements.   With head thrown back, and enormous bills resting on their breasts, they almost seem asleep.   A few easy strokes of their wings each minute, as their momentum or velocity diminishes, serves to keep them sustained at the same level.   The effort required is obviously slight, and not confirmatory of the excessive amount of power said to be requisite for maintaining the flight of a bird of this weight and size.   The pelican displays no symptom of being endowed with great strength, for when only slightly wounded it is easily captured, not having adequate power for effective resistance, but heavily flapping the huge wings, that should, as some imagine, give a stroke equal in vigour to the kick of a horse.

During a calm evening, flocks of spoonbills take their flight directly up the river's course; as if linked together in unison, and moved by the same impulse, they alter not their relative positions, but at less than fifteen inches above the water's surface, they speed swiftly by with ease and grace inimitable, a living sheet of spotless white.   Let one circumstance be remarked, — though they have fleeted past at a rate of near thirty miles an hour, so little do they disturb the element in which they move, that not a ripple of the placid bosom of the river, which they almost touch, has marked their track.   How wonderfully does their progress contrast with that of creatures who are compelled to drag their slow and weary way against the fluid a thousandfold more dense, flowing in strong and eddying current beneath them.

Our pennant droops listlessly, the wished-for north wind cometh not.   According to custom we step on shore, gun in hand.   A flock of white herons, or " buffalo-birds," almost within our reach, run a short distance from the pathway as we approach them.   Others are seen perched in social groups upon the backs of the apathetic and mud-begrimed animals whose name they bear.   Beyond the ripening dhourra crops which skirt the river-side, the land is covered with immense numbers of blue pigeons, flying to and fro in shoals, and searching for food with restless diligence.   The musical whistle from the pinions of the wood-doves sounds cheerily, as they dart past with the speed of an arrow. Ever and anon are seen a covey of the brilliant, many-coloured partridges of the district, whose *long and pointed wings* give them a strength and duration of flight that seems interminable, alighting at distances beyond the possibility of marking them down, as we are accustomed to do with their plumper brethren at home. But still more remarkable is the spectacle which the sky presents. As far as the eye can reach it is dotted with birds of prey of every size and description. Eagles, vultures, kites and hawks, of manifold species, down to the small, swallow-like, insectivorous hawk common in the Delta, which skims the surface of the ground in pursuit of its insect prey. None seem bent on going forward, but all are soaring leisurely round over the same locality, as if the invisible element which supports them were their medium of rest as well as motion. But mark that object sitting in solitary state in the midst of yon plain: what a magnificent eagle! An approach to within eighty yards arouses the king of birds from his apathy. He partly opens his enormous wings, but stirs not yet from his station. On gaining a few feet more he begins to *walk* away, with half-expanded, but motionless wings. Now for the chance fire! A charge of No. 3 from 11 bore rattles audibly but ineffectively upon his densely feathered body; his walk increases to a run, he gathers speed with his slowly-waving wings, and eventually leaves the ground. Rising at a gradual inclination, he mounts aloft and sails majestically away to his place of refuge in the Lybian range, distant at least five miles from where he rose. Some fragments of feathers denote the spot where the shot had struck him. The marks of his claws are traceable in the sandy soil, as, at first with firm and decided digs, he forced his way, but as he lightened his body and increased his speed with the aid of his wings, the imprints of his talons gradually merged into long scratches. The measured distance from the point where these vanished, to the place where he had stood, proved that with all the stimulus that the shot must have given to his exertions, he had been compelled to run full twenty yards before he could raise himself from the earth.

Again the boat is under weigh, though the wind is but just
sufficient to enable us to stem the current. An immense kite
is soaring overhead, scarcely higher than the top of our lateen
yard, affording a fine opportunity for contemplating his easy
and unlaboured movements. The cook has now thrown overboard some offal. With a solemn swoop the bird descends
and seizes it in his talons. How easily he rises again with
motionless expanded wings, the mere force and momentum of
his *descent* serving to raise him again to more than half-mast
high. Observe him next, with lazy flapping wings, and head
turned under his body; he is placidly devouring the pendant
morsel from his foot, and calmly gliding onwards.

The Nile abounds with large aquatic birds of almost every
variety. During a residence upon its surface for nine months
out of the year, immense numbers have been seen to come and
go, for the majority of them are migratory. Egypt being
merely a narrow strip of territory, passing through one of the
most desert parts of the earth, and rendered fertile only by the
periodical rise of the waters of the river, it is probable that
these birds make it their grand thoroughfare into the rich
districts of Central Africa.

On nearing our own shores, steaming against a moderate
head-wind, from a station abaft the wheel the movements of
some half-dozen gulls are observed, following in the wake of
the ship, in patient expectation of any edibles that may be
thrown overboard. One that is more familiar than the rest
comes so near at times that the winnowing of his wings can be
heard; he has just dropped astern, and now comes on again.
With the axis of his body exactly at the level of the eyesight,
his every movement can be distinctly marked. He approaches
to within ten yards, and utters his wild plaintive note, as he
turns his head from side to side, and regards us with his jet
black eye. But where is the angle or upward rise of his wings,
that should compensate for his descending tendency, in a yielding medium like air? The incline cannot be detected, for, to
all appearance, his wings are edgewise, or parallel to his line of
motion, and he appears to skim along a *solid* support. No

smooth-edged rails, or steel-tired wheels, with polished axles revolving in well oiled brasses, are needed here for the purpose of diminishing friction, for Nature's machinery has surpassed them all. The retarding effects of gravity in the creature under notice, are almost annulled, for he is gliding forward upon a *frictionless* plane. There are various reasons for concluding that the direct flight of many birds is maintained with a much less expenditure of power, for a high speed, than by any mode of progression.

The first subject for consideration is the proportion of surface to weight, and their combined effect in descending perpendicularly through the atmosphere. The datum is here based upon the consideration of *safety*, for it may sometimes be needful for a living being to drop passively, without muscular effort. One square foot of sustaining surface, for every pound of the total weight, will be sufficient for security.

According to Smeaton's table of atmospheric resistances, to produce a force of *one pound* on a square foot, the wind must move against the plane (or, which is the same thing, the plane against the wind), at the rate of twenty-two feet per second, or 1,320 feet per minute, equal to fifteen miles per hour. The resistance of the air will now balance the weight on the descending surface, and, consequently, it cannot exceed that speed. Now, twenty-two feet per second is the velocity acquired at the *end* of a fall of eight feet — a height from which a well-knit man or animal may leap down without much risk of injury. Therefore, if a man with parachute weigh together 143 lbs., spreading the same number of square feet of surface contained in a circle fourteen and a half feet in diameter, he will descend at perhaps an unpleasant velocity, but with safety to life and limb.

It is a remarkable fact how this proportion of wing-surface to weight extends throughout a great variety of the flying portion of the animal kingdom, even down to hornets, bees, and other insects. In some instances, however, as in the gallinaceous tribe, including pheasants, this area is somewhat exceeded, but they are known to be very poor flyers. Residing as they do chiefly on the ground, their wings are only required for short distances, or for raising them or easing their descent from their roosting-places in forest trees, the *shortness* of their wings preventing them from taking extended flights. The wing-surface of the common swallow is rather more than in the ratio of *two* square feet per pound, but having also great length of pinion, it is both swift and enduring in its flight. When on a rapid course this bird is in the habit of furling its wings into a narrow compass. The greater extent of surface is probably needful for the continual variations of speed and instant stoppages requisite for obtaining its insect food.

On the other hand, there are some birds, particularly of the duck tribe, whose wing-surface but little exceeds *half* a square foot, or sev.enty-two inches per pound, yet they may be classed among the strongest and swiftest of flyers. A weight of one pound, suspended from an area of this extent, would acquire a velocity due to a fall of 16 feet — a height sufficient for the destruction or injury of most animals. But when the plane is urged forward horizontally, in a manner analogous to the wings of a bird during flight, the sustaining power is greatly influenced by *the form and arrangement* of the surface.

In the case of *perpendicular* descent, as a parachute, the sustaining effect will be much the same, whatever the figure of the outline of the superficies may be, and a circle perhaps affords the best resistance of any. Take for example a circle of 20 square feet (as possessed by the pelican) loaded with as many pounds. This, as just stated, will limit the rate of perpendicular descent to 1,320 feet per minute. But instead of a circle 61 inches in diameter, if the area is bounded by a parallelogram 10 feet long by 2 feet broad, and whilst at perfect freedom to descend perpendicularly, let a force be applied exactly in a horizontal direction, so as to carry it edgeways, with the long side foremost, at a forward speed of 30 miles per hour — just double that of its passive descent: the rate of fall under these conditions will be decreased most remarkably, probably to less than $\frac{1}{15}$th part, or 88 feet per minute, or one mile per hour.

The annexed line represents transversely the plane 2 feet

wide and 10 feet long, moving in the direction of the arrow

with a forward speed of 30 miles per hour, or 2,640 feet per minute, and descending at 88 feet per minute, the ratio being as 1 to 30. Now, the particles of air, caught by the forward edge of the plane, must be carried down $\frac{8}{10}$ths of an inch before they leave it. This stratum, 10 feet wide and 2,640 long, will weigh not less than 134 lbs.; therefore the weight has continually to be moved downwards, 88 feet per minute, from a state of absolute rest. If the plane, with this weight and an upward rise of $\frac{8}{10}$ths of an inch, be carried forward at a rate of 30 miles per hour, it will be maintained at the same level without descending.

The following illustrations, though referring to the action of surfaces in a denser fluid, are yet exactly analogous to the conditions set forth in air : —

Take a stiff rod of wood, and nail to its end at right angles a thin lath or blade, about two inches wide. Place the rod square across the thwarts of a rowing-boat in motion, letting a foot or more of the blade hang perpendicularly over the side into the water. The direct amount of resistance of the current against the flat side of the blade may thus be felt. Next slide the rod to and fro thwart ship, keeping all square ; the resistance will now be found to have increased enormously ; indeed, the boat can be entirely stopped by such an appliance. Of course the same experiment may be tried in a running stream.

Another familiar example may be cited in the lee-boards and sliding keels used in vessels of shadow draught, *which act precisely on the same principle as the plane or wing-surface of a bird when moving in air.* These surfaces, though parallel to the line of the vessel's course, enable her to carry a heavy press of sail without giving way under the side pressure, or making lee-way, so great is their resistance against the rapidly passing body of water, which cannot be deflected sideways at a high speed.

The succeeding experiments will serve further to exemplify

the action of the same principle. Fix a thin blade, say one
inch wide and one foot long, with its plane exactly midway and
at right angles, to the end of a spindle or rod. On thrusting
this through a body of water, or immersing it in a stream running in the direction of the axis of the spindle, the resistance
will be simply that caused by the water against the mere superficies of the blade. Next put the spindle and blade in rapid
rotation. The retarding effect against direct motion will now be
increased near *tenfold*, and is equal to that due *to the entire area
of the circle of revolution*. By trying the effect of blades of
various widths, it will be found that, for the purpose of effecting the maximum amount of resistance, the more rapidly the
spindle revolves the narrower may be the blade. There is a
specific ratio between the *width* of the blade and its *velocity*.
It is of some importance that this should be precisely defined,
not only for its practical utility in determining the best proportion of width to speed in the blades of screw-propellers, but
also for a correct demonstration of the principles involved in
the subject now under consideration; for it may be remarked
that the swiftest-flying birds possess extremely long and *narrow*
wings, and the slow, heavy flyers short and wide ones.

In the early days of the screw-propeller, it was thought
requisite, in order to obtain the advantage of the utmost extent
of surface, that the end-view of the screw should present no
opening, but appear as a complete disc. Accordingly, some
were constructed with one or two threads, making an entire or two
half-revolutions; but this was subsequently found to be a mistake. In the case of the two blades, the length of the screw
was shortened, and consequently the width of the blades reduced, with increased effect, till each was brought down to
considerably less than *one-sixth* of the circumference or area
of the entire circle; the maximum speed was then obtained.
Experiment has also shown that the effective propelling area of
the two-bladed screw is tantamount to its entire circle of revolution, and is generally estimated as such.

Many experiments tried by the author, with various forms of
screws, applied to a small steam-boat, led to the same conclu-

sion — that the two blades of one-sixth of the circle gave the best result.

All screws reacting on a fluid such as water, must cause it to yield to some extent; this is technically known as "slip," and whatever the ratio or per-centage on the speed of the boat may be, it is tantamount to *just so much loss of propelling power* — this being consumed in giving motion to the water instead of the boat.

On starting the engine of the steam-boat referred to, and grasping a mooring-rope at the stern, it was an easy matter to hold it back with one hand, though the engine was equal in power to five horses, and the screw making more than 500 revolutions per minute. The whole force of the steam was absorbed in "slip," or in giving motion to the column of water; but let her go, and allow the screw to find an abutment on a fresh body of water, not having received a gradual motion, and with its *inertia undisturbed* when running under full way, the screw worked almost as if in a solid nut, the "slip" amounting to only eleven per cent.

The laws which control the action of inclined surfaces, moving either in straight lines or circles in *air*, are identical, and serve to show the inutility of attempting to raise a heavy body in the atmosphere by means of rotating vanes or a screw acting vertically; for unless the ratio of surface compared to weight is exceedingly extensive, the whole power will be consumed in "slip," or in giving a downward motion to the column of air. Even if a sufficient force is obtained to keep a body suspended by such means, yet, after the desired altitude is arrived at, *no further ascension* is required; there the apparatus is to remain stationary as to level, and its position on the constantly yielding support can only be maintained at an enormous expenditure of power, for the screw cannot obtain a hold upon a *fresh and unmoved* portion of air in the same manner as it does upon the body of water when propelling the boat at full speed; its action under these conditions is the same as when the boat is held fast, in which case, although the engine is working up to its usual rate, the tractive power is almost annulled.

Some experiments made with a screw, or pair of inclined vanes acting vertically in air, were tried, in the following manner. To an upright post was fixed a frame, containing a bevil wheel and pinion, multiplying in the ratio of three to one. The axle of the wheel was horizontal, and turned by a handle of five-and-a-half inches radius. The spindle of the pinion rotated vertically, and carried two driving-pins at the end of a cross-piece, so that the top resembled the three prongs of a trident. The upright shaft of the screw was bored hollow to receive the middle prong, while the two outside ones took a bearing against a driving-bar, at right angles to the lower end of the shaft, the top of which ended in a long iron pivot, running in a socket fixed in a beam overhead; it could thus rise and fall about two inches with very little friction. The top of the screw-shaft carried a cross-arm, with a blade of equal size at each extremity, the distance from end to end being six feet. The blades could be adjusted at any angle by clamping-screws. Both their edges, and the arms that carried them, were bevilled away to a sharp edge to diminish the effects of atmospheric resistance. A wire stay was taken from the base of each blade to the bottom of the upright shaft, to give rigidity to the arms, and to prevent them from springing upwards. With this apparatus experiments were made with weights attached to the upright screw-shaft, and the blades set at different pitches, or angles of inclination. When the vanes were rotated rapidly, they rose and floated on the air, carrying the weights with them. Much difficulty was experienced in raising a heavy weight by a comparatively small extent of surface, moving at a high velocity; the "slip" in these cases being so great as to absorb all the power employed. The utmost effect obtained in this way was to raise a weight of six pounds on one square foot of sustaining surface, the planes having been set at a coarse pitch. To keep up the rotation, required about half the power a man could exert.

The ratio of weight to sustaining surface was next arranged in the proportion approximating to that of birds. Two of the experiments are here quoted, which gave the most satisfactory result. Weight of wings and shaft, $17\frac{1}{2}$ oz.; area of two wings, 121 inches — equal to 110 square inches per pound. The annexed figures are given approximately, in order to avoid decimal fractions: —

	No. of revolutions per minute.	Mean sustaining speed. Miles per hour.	Feet per minute.	Pitch or angle of rise in one revolution. Inches.	Ratio of pitch to speed.	Slip per cent.
1st Experiment.	210	38	3,360	26	$\frac{1}{8}$th nearly	$12\frac{1}{2}$
2nd Do.	240	44	3,840	15	$\frac{1}{13}$th Do.	8

The power required to drive was nearly the same in both experiments — about equal to one-sixteenth part of a horse-power, or the third part of the strength of a man, as estimated by a constant force on the handle of twelve pounds in the first experiment, and ten in the second, the radius of the handle being five-and-a-half inches, and making seventy revolutions per minute in the first case, and eighty in the other.

These experiments are so far satisfactory in showing the small pitch or angle of rise required for sustaining the weight stated, and demonstrating the principle before alluded to, of the slow descent of planes moving horizontally in the atmosphere at high velocities; but the question remains to be answered, concerning the disposal of the excessive power consumed in raising a weight not exceeding that of a carrier pigeon, for unless this can be satisfactorily accounted for, there is but little prospect of finding an available power, of sufficient energy in its application to the mechanism, for raising apparatus, either experimental or otherwise, in the atmosphere. In the second experiment, the screw-shaft made 240 revolutions, consequently, one vane (there being two) was constantly passing over the *same spot* 480 times each minute, or eight times in a second. This caused a descending current of air, moving at the rate of near four miles per hour, almost sufficient to blow a candle out placed three feet underneath. This is the result of " slip," and

the giving both a downward and rotary motion to this column
of air, will account for a great part of the power employed, as
the whole apparatus performed the work of a blower.   If the
wings, instead of travelling in a circle, could have been urged
continually forward in a straight line in a fresh and unmoved
body of air the " slip " would have been so inconsiderable, and
the pitch consequently, reduced to such a small angle, as to
add but little to the direct forward atmospheric resistance of
the edge.

The small flying screws, sold as toys, are well known.   It is
an easy matter to determine approximately the force expended
in raising and maintaining them in the atmosphere.   The following is an example of one constructed of tin-plate with three
equidistant vanes.   This was spun by means of a cord, wound
round a wooden spindle, fitted into a forked handle as usual.
The outer end of the coiled string was attached to a small
spring steelyard, which served as a handle to pull it out by.   The
weight, or degree at which the index had been drawn, was *afterwards* ascertained by the mark left thereon by a pointed brass
wire.   It is not necessary to know the *time* occupied in drawing out the string, as this item in the estimate may be taken as
the duration of the ascent; for it is evident that if the same
force is re-applied at the descent, it would rise again, and a
repeated series of these impulses will represent the power required to prolong the flight of the instrument.   It is, therefore,
requisite to know the length of string, and the force applied in
pulling it out.   The following are the data : —

Diameter of screw   .   .   .   .   .   .   8½ inches.
Weight of ditto .   .   .   . 396 grains.
Length of string drawn out .   .   .   .   .   2 feet.
Force employed .   .   .   .   8 lbs.
Duration of flight   .   .   .   .   .   . 16 seconds.

From this it may be computed that, in order to maintain the
flight of the instrument, a constant force is required of near
sixty foot-pounds per minute — in the ratio of about three

horse-power for each hundred pounds raised by such means. The force is perhaps over-estimated for a larger screw, for as the size and weight is increased, the power required would be less than in this ratio. The result would be more satisfactory if tried with a sheet-iron screw, impelled by a descending weight.

Methods analogous to this have been proposed for attempting aerial locomotion; but experiment has shown that a screw rotating in the air is an imperfect principle for obtaining the means of flight, and supporting the needful weight, for the power required is enormous. Suppose a machine to be constructed, having some adequate supply of force, the screw rotating vertically at a certain velocity will raise the whole. When the desired altitude is obtained, nearly the same velocity of revolution, and the same excessive power, must be continued, and consumed *entirely in* " *slip*," or in drawing down a rapid current of air.

If the axis of the screw is slightly inclined from the perpendicular, the whole machine will travel forward. The "slip," and consequently the power, is somewhat reduced under these conditions; but a swift forward speed cannot be effected by such means, for the resistance of the inclined disc of the screw will be very great, far exceeding any form assimilating to the edge of the wing of a bird. But, arguing on the supposition that a forward speed of thirty miles an hour might thus be obtained, even then nearly all the power would be expended in giving an unnecessary and rapid revolution to an immense screw, capable of raising a weight, say of 200 pounds. The weight alone of such a machine must cause it to fail, and every revolution of the screw is a subtraction from the much-desired direct forward speed. A simple narrow blade, or inclined plane, propelled in a direct course at *this* speed — which is amply sufficient for sustaining heavy weights — is the best, and, in fact, the only means of giving the maximum amount of supporting power with the least possible degree of " slip," and direct forward resistance. Thousands of examples in Nature testify its success, and show the principle in perfection; — apparently the only one, and therefore beyond the reach of amendment, the wing of a bird, combining a propelling and supporting organ in one, each perfectly efficient in its mechanical action.

This leads to the consideration of the amount of power requisite to maintain the flight of a bird. Anatomists state that the pectoral muscles for giving motion to the wings are excessively large and strong; but this furnishes no proof of the expenditure of a great amount of force in the act of flying. The wings are hinged to the body like two powerful levers, and some counteracting force of a *passive* nature, acting like a spring under tension, must be requisite merely to balance the weight of the bird. It cannot be shown that, while there is no active motion, there is any real exertion of muscular force; for instance, during the time when a bird is soaring with motionless wings. This must be considered as a state of equilibrium, the downward spring and elasticity of the wings serving to support the body; the muscles, in such a case, performing like stretched india-rubber springs would do. The motion or active power required for the performance of flight must be considered exclusive of this.

It is difficult, if not impossible, by any form of dynamometer, to ascertain the precise amount of force given out by the wings of birds; but this is perhaps not requisite in proof of the principle involved, for when the laws governing their movements in air are better understood, it is quite possible to demonstrate, by isolated experiments, the amount of power required to sus-tain and propel a given weight and surface at any speed.

If the pelican referred to as weighing twenty-one pounds, with near the same amount of wing-area in square feet, were to descend perpendicularly, it would fall at the rate of 1,320 feet per minute, being limited to this speed by the resistance of the atmosphere.

The standard generally employed in estimating power is by the rate of descent of a weight. Therefore, the weight of the bird being 21 pounds, which, falling at the above speed will expend a force on the air set in motion nearly equal to one horse (.84 HP.) or that of 5 men; and conversely, to raise this weight again perpendicularly upon a yielding support like air, would require even more power than this expression, which it is certain that a pelican does not possess; nor does it appear that any *large* bird has the faculty of raising itself on the wing *perpendicularly* in a still atmosphere. A pigeon is able to accomplish this nearly, mounting to the top of a house in a very narrow compass; but the exertion is evidently severe, and can only be maintained for a short period. For its size, this bird has great power of wing; but this is perhaps far exceeded in the humming-bird, which, by the extremely rapid movements of its pinions, sustains itself for more than a minute in still air in one position. The muscular force required for this feat is much greater than for any other performance of flight. The body of the bird at the time is nearly vertical. The wings uphold the weight, not by striking vertically downwards upon the air, but as inclined surfaces reciprocating horizontally like a screw, but wanting in its continuous rotation in one direction, and, in consequence of the loss arising from rapid alternations of motion, the power required for the flight will exceed that specified in the screw experiment before quoted, viz.: three horse-power for every 100 pounds raised.

We have here an example of the exertion of enormous animal force expended in flight, necessary for the peculiar habits of the bird, and for obtaining its food; but in the other extreme, in large heavy birds, whose wings are merely required for the purposes of migration or locomotion, flight is obtained with the least possible degree of power, and this condition can only be commanded by a rapid straightforward course through the air.

The sustaining power obtained in flight must depend upon certain laws of action and reaction between relative weights; the weight of a bird, balanced, or finding an abutment, against the fixed inertia of a far greater weight of air, continuously brought into action in a given time. This condition is secured, not by extensive surface, but by great length of wing, which, in forward motion, takes a support upon a wide stratum of air, extending transversely to the line of direction.

The pelican, for example, has wings extending out 10 feet. If the limits of motion imparted to the substratum of air, acted upon by the incline of the wing, be assumed as one foot in thickness, and the velocity of flight as 30 miles per hour, or 2,640 feet per minute, the stratum of air passed over in this time will weigh nearly one ton, or 100 times the weight of the body of the bird, thus giving such an enormous supporting power, that the comparatively small weight of the bird has but little effect in deflecting the heavy length of stratum downwards, and, therefore, the higher the velocity of flight the less the amount of " slip," or power wasted in compensation for descent.

As noticed at the commencement of this paper, large birds may be observed to skim close above smooth water without ruffling the surface; showing that during rapid flight the air does not give way beneath them, but approximates towards a solid support.

In all inclined surfaces, moving rapidly through air, the whole sustaining power approaches toward the front edge; and in order to exemplify the inutility of surface alone, without proportionate length of wing, take a plane, ten feet long by two broad, impelled with the narrow end forward, the first twelve or fifteen inches will be as efficient at a high speed in supporting a weight as the entire following portion of the plane, which may be cut off, thus reducing the effective wing-area of a pelican, arranged in this direction, to the totally inadequate equivalent of two-and-a-half square feet.

One of the most perfect natural examples of easy and long-sustained flight is the wandering albatross. " A bird for endurance of flight probably unrivalled. Found over all parts of the Southern Ocean, it seldom rests on the water. During storms, even the most terrific, it is seen now dashing through the whirling clouds, and now serenely floating, without the least observable motion of its outstretched pinions." The wings of this bird extend fourteen or fifteen feet from end to end, and measure only eight-and-a-half inches across the broadest part. This conformation gives the bird such an extraordinary sustaining power, that it is said to *sleep* on the wing during stormy weather, when rest on the ocean is impossible. Rising high in the air, it skims slowly down, with absolutely motionless wings, till a near approach to the waves awakens it, when it rises again for another rest.

If the force expended in actually sustaining a long-winged bird upon a wide and unyielding stratum of air, during rapid flight, is but a small fraction of its strength, then nearly the whole is exerted in overcoming direct forward resistance. In the pelican referred to, the area of the body, at its greatest diameter, is about 100 square inches; that of the pinions, eighty. But as the contour of many birds during flight approximates nearly to Newton's solid of least resistance, by reason of this form, acting like the sharp bows of a ship, the opposing force against the wind must be reduced down to one third or fourth part; this gives one-tenth of a horse-power, or about half the strength of a man, expended during a flight of thirty miles per hour. Judging from the action of the living bird when captured, it does not appear to be more powerful than here stated.

The transverse area of a carrier pigeon during flight (including the outstretched wings) a little exceeds the ratio of twelve square inches for each pound, and the wing-surface, or sustaining area, ninety square inches per pound.

Experiments have been made to test the resisting power of conical bodies of various forms, in the following manner: — A thin lath was placed horizontally, so as to move freely on a pivot set midway; at one end of the lath a circular card was attached, at the other end a sliding clip traversed, for holding paper cones, having their bases the exact size of the opposite disc. The instrument acted like a steelyard; and when held against the wind, the paper cones were adjusted at different distances from the centre, according to their forms and angles, in order to balance the resistance of the air against the opposing flat surface. The resistance was found to be diminished nearly in the ratio that the height of the cone exceeded the diameter of base.

It might be expected that the pull of the string of a flying kite should give some indication of the force of inclined surfaces acting against a current of air; but no correct data can be obtained in this way. The incline of the kite is far greater than ever appears in the case of the advancing wing-surface of a bird. The tail is purposely made to give steadiness by a strong pull backwards from the action of the wind, which also exerts considerable force on the suspended cord, which for more than half its length hangs nearly perpendicularly. But the kite, as a means of obtaining unlimited lifting and tractive power, in certain cases where it might be usefully applied, seems to have been somewhat neglected. For its power of raising weights, the following quotation is taken from Vol. XLI. of the *Transactions of the Society of Arts*, relating to Captain Dansey's mode of communicating with a lee-shore. The kite was made of a sheet of holland exactly nine feet square, extended by two spars placed diagonally, and as stretched spread a surface of fifty-five square feet. "The kite, in a strong breeze, extended 1,100 yards of line five-eighths in circumference, and would have extended more had it been at hand. It also extended 360 yards of line, one and three-quarters of an inch in circumference, weighing sixty pounds. The holland weighed three and a half pounds; the spars, one of which was armed at the head with iron spikes, for the purpose of mooring it, six and three-quarter pounds; and the tail was five times its length, composed of eight pounds of rope and fourteen of elm plank, weighing together twenty-two pounds."

We have here the remarkable fact of ninety-two and a quarter pounds carried by a surface of only fifty-five square feet.

As all such experiments bear a very close relation to the subject of this paper, it may be suggested that a form of kite should be employed for reconnoitring and exploring purposes, in lieu of balloons held by ropes. These would be torn to pieces in the very breeze that would render a kite most serviceable and safe. In the arrangement there should be a smaller and upper kite, capable of sustaining the weight of the apparatus. The lower kite should be as nearly as practicable in the form of a circular flat plane, distended with ribs, with a car attached beneath like a parachute. Four guy-ropes leading to the car would be required for altering the angle of the plane — vertically with respect to the horizon, and laterally relative to the direction of the wind. By these means the observer could regulate his altitude, so as to command a view of a country, in a radius of at least twenty miles; he could veer to a great extent from side to side, from the wind's course, or lower himself gently, with the choice of a suitable spot for descent. Should the cord break, or the wind fail, the kite would, in either case, act as a parachute, and as such might be purposely detached from the cord, which then being sustained from the upper kite, could be easily recovered. The direction of descent could be commanded by the guy-ropes, these being hauled taut in the required direction for landing.

The author has good reasons for believing that there would be less risk associated with the employment of this apparatus, than the reconnoitring balloons that have now frequently been made use of in warfare.[1]

---

[1] The practical application of these suggestions appears to have been anticipated some years previously. In a small work, styled the "History of the Charvolant, or Kite Carriage," published by Longman and Co., appear the following remarks : — "These buoyant sails, possessing immense power, will, as we have before remarked, serve for floating observatories. . . . Elevated in the air, a single sentinel, with a perspective, could watch and report the advance of the most powerful forces, while yet at a great distance. He could mark their line of march, the composition of their force, and their general strength, long before he could be seen by the enemy." Again, at page 53, we have an account of ascents actually made, as follows : — "Nor was less progress made in the experimental department, when large weights were required to be raised or transposed. While on this subject, we must not omit to observe that the first person who soared aloft in the air by this invention was a lady, whose courage would not be denied this test of its strength. An arm-chair was brought on the ground, then lowering the cordage of the kite by slackening the lower brace, the chair was firmly lashed to the mainline, and the lady took her seat. The main-brace being hauled taut, the huge buoyant sail rose aloft with its fair burden, continuing to ascend to the height of 100 yards. On descending, she expressed herself much pleased with the easy motion of the kite, and the delightful prospect she had enjoyed. Soon after this, another experiment of a similar nature took place, when the inventor's son successfully carried out a design not less safe than bold; that of scaling, by this powerful aërial machine, the brow of a cliff 200 feet in perpendicular height. Here, after safely landing, he again took his seat in a chair expressly prepared for the purpose, and, detaching the swivel-line, which kept it at its elevation, glided gently down the cordage to the hand of the director. The buoyant sail employed on this occasion was thirty feet in height, with a proportionate spread of canvas. The rise of the machine was most majestic, and nothing could surpass the steadiness with which it was manœuvred; the certainty with which it answered the action of the braces, and the ease with which its power was lessened or increased. . . . Subsequently to this, an experiment of a very bold and novel character

The wings of all flying creatures, whether of birds, bats, butterflies, or other insects, have this one peculiarity of structure in common. The front, or leading edge, is rendered rigid by bone, cartilage, or a thickening of the membrane; and in most birds of perfect flight, even the individual feathers are formed upon the same condition. In consequence of this, when the wing is waved in air, it gives a persistent force in one direction, caused by the elastic reaction of the following portion of the edge. The fins and tails of fishes act upon the same principle. In the most rapid swimmers these organs are termed "lobated and pointed." The tail extends out very wide transversely to the body, so that a powerful impulse is obtained against a wide stratum of water, on the condition before explained. This action is imitated in Macintosh's screw-propeller, the blade of which is made of thin steel, so as to be elastic. While the vessel is stationary, the blades are in a line with the keel, but during rotation they bend on one side, more or less, according to the speed and degree of propulsion required, and are thus self-compensating; and could practical difficulties be overcome, would prove to be a form of propeller perfect in theory.

In the flying mechanism of beetles there is a difference of arrangement. When the elytra, or wing-cases, are opened, they are checked by a stop, which sets them at a fixed angle. It is probable that these serve as "aeroplanes," for carrying the weight of the insect, while the delicate membrane that folds beneath acts more as a propelling than a supporting organ. A beetle cannot fly with the elytra removed.

The wing of a bird, or bat, is both a supporting and propel-

was made upon an extensive down, where a wagon with a considerable load was drawn along, whilst this huge machine, at the same time, carried an observer aloft in the air, realising almost the romance of flying."

It may be remarked that the brace-lines here referred to were conveyed down the main-line and managed below; but it is evident that the same lines could be managed with equal facility by the person seated in the car above; and if the main-line were attached to a water-drag instead of a wheeled car, the adventurer could cross rivers, lakes, or bays, with considerable latitude for steering and selecting the point of landing, by hauling on the port or starboard brace-lines as required. And from the uniformity of the resistance offered by the water-drag, this experiment could not be attended with any greater amount of risk than a land flight by the same means.

ling organ, and flight is performed in a rapid course, as follows: — During the down-stroke it can be easily imagined how the bird is sustained; but in the up-stroke, the weight is also equally well supported, for in raising the wing, it is slightly inclined upwards against the rapidly passing air, and as this angle is somewhat in excess of the motion due to the raising of the wing, the bird is sustained as much during the up as the down-stroke — in fact, though the wing may be rising, the bird is still pressing against the air with a force equal to the weight of its body. The faculty of turning up the wing may be easily seen when a large bird alights; for after gliding down its aerial gradient, on its approach to the ground it turns up the plane of its wing against the air; this checks its descent, and it lands gently.

It has before been shown how utterly inadequate the mere perpendicular impulse of a plane is found to be in supporting a weight, when there is no horizontal motion at the time. There is no material weight of air to be acted upon, and it yields to the slightest force, however great the velocity of impulse may be. On the other hand, suppose that a large bird, in full flight, can make forty miles per hour, or 3,520 feet per minute, and performs one stroke per second. Now, during every fractional portion of that stroke, the wing is acting upon and obtaining an impulse from a fresh and undisturbed body of air; and if the vibration of the wing is limited to an arc of two feet, this by no means represents the small force of action that would be obtained when in a stationary position, for the impulse is secured upon a stratum of fifty-eight feet in length of air at each stroke. So that the conditions of weight of air for obtaining support equally well apply to weight of air, and its reaction in producing forward impulse.

So necessary is the acquirement of this horizontal speed, even in commencing flight, that most heavy birds, when possible, rise against the wind, and even run at the top of their speed to make their wings available, as in the example of the eagle, mentioned at the commencement of this paper. It is stated that the Arabs, on horseback, can approach near enough to spear these birds, when on the plain, before they are able to rise: their habit is to perch on an eminence, where possible.

The tail of a bird is not necessary for flight. A pigeon can fly perfectly with this appendage cut short off: it probably performs an important function in steering, for it is to be remarked, that most birds that have either to pursue or evade pursuit are amply provided with this organ.

The foregoing reasoning is based upon facts, which tend to show that the flight of the largest and heaviest of all birds is really performed with but a small amount of force, and that man is endowed with sufficient muscular power to enable him also to take individual and extended flights, and that success is probably only involved in a question of suitable mechanical adaptations. But if the wings are to be modelled in imitation of natural examples, but very little consideration will serve to demonstrate its utter impracticability when applied in these forms. The annexed diagram, Fig. 1, would be about the proportions needed for a man of medium weight. The wings, *a a*, must extend out sixty feet from end to end, and measure four feet across the broadest part. The man, *b*, should be in a horizontal position, encased in a strong framework, to which the wings are hinged at *c c*. The wings must be stiffened by elastic ribs, extending back from the pinions. These must be trussed by a thin band of steel, *e e*, Fig. 2, for the purpose of diminishing the weight and thickness of the spar. At the front, where the pinions are hinged, there are two levers attached, and drawn together by a spiral spring, *d*, Fig. 2, the tension of which is sufficient to balance the weight of the body and machine, and cause the wings to be easily vibrated by the movement of the feet acting on treadles. This spring serves the purpose of the pectoral muscles in birds. But with all such arrangements the apparatus must fail — *length of wing is indispensable!* and a spar thirty feet long must be strong, heavy, and cumbrous; to propel this alone through the air, at a high speed, would require more power than any man could command.

In repudiating all imitations of natural wings, it does not follow that the only channel is closed in which flying mechanism

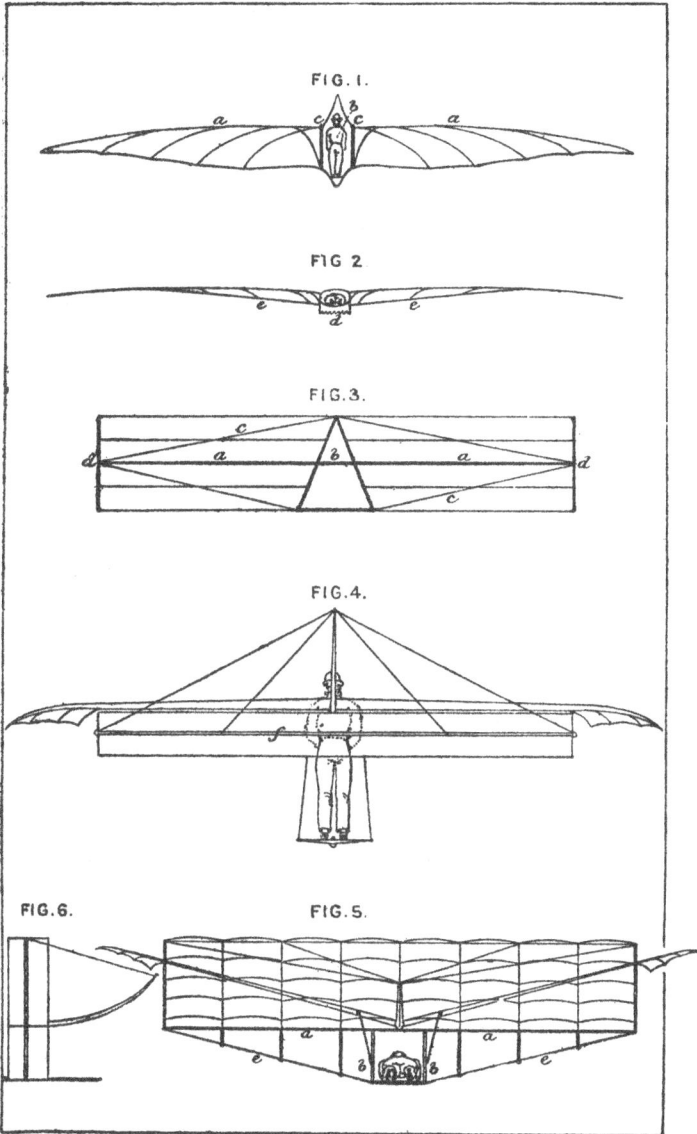

FIG. 1.

FIG 2

FIG. 3.

FIG. 4.

FIG. 6.

FIG. 5.

may prove successful.   Though birds do fly upon definite mechanical principles, and with a moderate exertion of force, yet the wing must necessarily be a vital organ and member of the living body. It must have a marvellous self-acting principle of repair, in case the feathers are broken or torn; it must also fold up in a small compass, and form a covering for the body.

These considerations bear no relation to artificial wings; so in designing a flying-machine, any deviations are admissible, provided the theoretical conditions involved in flight are borne in mind.

Having remarked how thin a stratum of air is displaced beneath the wings of a bird in rapid flight, it follows that in order to obtain the necessary *length* of plane of supporting heavy weights, the surfaces may be superposed, or placed in parallel rows, with an interval between them.   A dozen pelicans may fly one above the other without mutual impediment, as if framed together; and it is thus shown how two hundred weight may be supported in a transverse distance of only ten feet.

In order to test this idea, six bands of stiff paper, three feet long and three inches wide, were stretched at a slight upward angle, in a light rectangular frame, with an interval of three inches between them, the arrangement resembling an open Venetian blind.   When this was held against a breeze, the lifting power was very great, and even by running with it in a calm it required much force to keep it down.   The success of this model led to the construction of one of a sufficient size to carry the weight of a man. Fig. 3 represents the arrangement. *a a* is a thin plank, tapered at the outer ends, and attached at the base to a triangle, *b*, made of similar plank, for the insertion of the body. The boards, *a a*, were trussed with thin bands of iron, *c c*, and at the ends were vertical rods, *d d*.   Between these were stretched five bands of holland, fifteen inches broad and sixteen feet long, the total length of the web being eighty feet.   This was taken out after dark into a wet piece of meadow land, one November evening, during a strong breeze, wherein it became quite unmanageable. The wind acting upon the already tightly-stretched webs, their united pull caused the central boards to bend considerably, with a twisting, vibratory motion. During a lull, the head and shoulders were inserted in the triangle, with the chest resting on the base board. A sudden gust caught up the experimenter, who was carried some distance from the ground, and the affair falling over sideways, broke up the right-hand set of webs.

In all new machines we gain experience by repeated failures, which frequently form the stepping-stones to ultimate success. The rude contrivance just described (which was but the work of a few hours) had taught, first, that the webs, or aeroplanes, must not be distended in a frame, as this must of necessity be strong and heavy, to withstand their combined tension; second, that the planes must be made so as either to furl or fold up, for the sake of portability.

In order to meet these conditions, the following arrangement was afterwards tried: — *a a*, Figs. 4 and 5, is the main spar, sixteen feet long, half an inch thick at the base, and tapered, both in breadth and thickness, to the end; to this spar was fastened the panels *b b*, having a base-board for the support of the body. Under this, and fastened to the end of the main spar, is a thin steel tie-band, *e e*, with struts starting from the spar. This served as the foundation of the superposed aeroplanes, and, though very light, was found to be exceedingly strong; for when the ends of the spar were placed upon supports, the middle bore the weight of the body without any strain or deflection; and further, by a separation at the base-board, the spars could be folded back, with a hinge, to half their length. Above this were arranged the aeroplanes, consisting of six webs of thin holland, fifteen inches broad; these were kept in parallel planes, by vertical divisions, two feet wide, of the same fabric, so that when distended by a current of air, each two feet of web pulled in opposition to its neighbour; and finally, at the ends (which were each sewn over laths), a pull due to only two feet had to be counteracted, instead of the strain arising from the entire length, as in the former experiment. The end-pull was sustained by vertical rods, sliding through loops on the transverse ones at the ends of the webs, the whole of which could fall flat on the spar, till raised and distended by a breeze. The top was stretched by a lath, *f*, and the system kept vertical by staycords, taken from a bowsprit carried out in front, shown in Fig. 6. All the front edges of the aeroplanes were stiffened by bands of crinoline steel. This series was for the supporting arrangement, being equivalent to a length of wing of ninety-six feet. Exterior to this, two propellers were to be attached, turning on spindles just above the back. They are kept drawn up by a light spring, and pulled down by cords or chains, running over pulleys in the panels *b b*, and fastened to the end of a swivelling cross-yoke, sliding on the base-board. By working this cross-piece with the feet, motion will be communicated to the propellers, and by giving a longer stroke with one foot than the other, a greater extent of motion will be given to the corresponding propeller, thus enabling the machine to turn, just as oars are worked in a rowing boat. The propellers act on the same principle as the wing of a bird or bat: their ends being made of fabric, stretched by elastic ribs, a simple waving motion up and down will give a strong forward impulse. In order to start, the legs are lowered beneath the base-board, and the experimenter must run against the wind.

An experiment recently made with this apparatus developed a cause of failure. The angle required for producing the requisite supporting power was found to be so small, that the crinoline steel would not keep the front edges in tension. Some of them were borne downwards and more on one side than the other, by the operation of the wind, and this also produced a strong fluttering motion in the webs, destroying the integrity of their plane surfaces, and fatal to their proper action.

Another arrangement has since been constructed, having laths sewn in both edges of the webs, which are kept permanently distended by cross-stretchers. All these planes are hinged to a vertical central board, so as to fold back when the bottom ties are released, but the system is much heavier than the former one, and no experiments of any consequence have as yet been tried with it.

It may be remarked that although a principle is here defined, yet considerable difficulty is experienced in carrying the theory into practice. When the wind approaches to fifteen or twenty miles per hour, the lifting power of these arrangements is all that is requisite, and, by additional planes, can be increased to any extent; but the capricious nature of the ground-currents is a perpetual source of trouble.

Great weight does not appear to be of much consequence, *if carried in the body;* but the aeroplanes and their attachments seem as if they were required to be very light, otherwise, they are awkward to carry, and impede the movements in running and making a start. In a dead calm, it is almost impracticable to get sufficient horizontal speed, by *mere running* alone, to raise the weight of the body. Once off the ground, the speed must be an increasing one, if continued by suitable propellers. The small amount of experience as yet gained, appears to indicate that if the aeroplanes could be raised in detail, like a superposed series of kites, they would first carry the weight of the machine itself, and next relieve that of the body.

Until the last few months no substantial attempt has been made to construct a flying-machine, in accordance with the principle involved in this paper, which was written seven years ago. The author trusts that he has contributed something towards the elucidation of a new theory, and shown that the flight of a bird in its performance does not require that enormous amount of force usually supposed, and that in fact birds do not exert more power in flying than quadrupeds in running, but considerably less; for the wing movements of a large bird, travelling at a far higher speed in air, are very much slower; and, where weight is concerned, great velocity of action in the locomotive organs is associated with great force.

It is to be hoped that further experiments will confirm the correctness of these observations, and with a sound working theory upon which to base his operations, man may yet command the air with the same facility that birds now do.

The CHAIRMAN: " I think the paper just read is one of great interest and importance, especially as it points out the true mechanical explanation of the curious problem, as to how and why it is that birds of the most powerful flight always have the longest and narrowest wings. I think it quite certain, that if the air is ever to be navigated, it will not be by individual men flying by means of machinery; but that it is quite possible vessels may be invented, which will carry a number of men, and the motive force of which will not be muscular action. We must first ascertain clearly the mechanical principles upon which flight is achieved; and this is a subject which has scarcely ever been investigated in a scientific spirit. In fact, you will see in our best works of science, by the most distinguished men, the account given of the anatomy of birds is, that a bird flies by inflating itself with warm air, by which it becomes buoyant, like a balloon. The fact is, however, that a bird is never buoyant. A bird is immensely heavier than the air. We all know that the moment a bird is shot it falls to the earth; and it must necessarily do so, because one of the essential mechanical principles of flight is weight, without it there can be no momentum, and no motive force capable of moving through atmospheric currents.

"Until I read Mr. Wenham's paper, a few weeks since, I was puzzled by the fact, that birds with long and very narrow wings seem to be not only as efficient fliers, but much more efficient fliers than birds with very large, broad wings. If you observe the flight of the common heron — which is a bird with a very large wing, disposed rather in breadth than in length — you will notice that it is exceedingly slow, and that it has a very heavy, flapping motion. The common swallow, on the other hand, is provided with a long and narrow wing, and I never understood how it was that long-winged birds, such as these, achieved so rapid a flight, until I read Mr. Wenham's paper. Although I do not profess to be able to follow the elaborate calculations which he has laid before us, I think I now understand the explanation he has given. His explanation of the action of narrow wings upon the air is, that it is precisely like the action of the narrow vanes of the ship's screw in water, and that the resisting power of the screw is the same, or nearly the same, whether you have the total area of revolution covered by solid surface, or traversed by long and narrow vanes in rotation.

" If Mr. Wenham's explanation be nearly correct, that supposing this implement (referring to a model) to be carried forward by some propelling power, the sustaining force of the whole area is simply the sustaining force of the narrow band in front. This, however, is a matter which will have to be decided by experiment. It certainly appears to explain the phenomena of the flight of birds. There are one or two observations in the paper I do not quite agree with. Although I have studied the subject for many years, I have not arrived at Mr. Wenham's conclusion that the upward stroke of a bird's wing has precisely the same effect as a downward stroke in sustaining. An upward stroke has a contrary effect to the downward stroke; it has a propelling power certainly, but I believe that the sustaining power of a bird's flight is due entirely to the downward stroke. I should be glad to hear what Mr. Wenham may have to say upon this. My belief is, that an upward stroke must have, so far as sustaining is concerned, a reverse action to the downward stroke.

" Then with regard to another observation of Mr. Wenham's, that the tails of birds are used as rudders. I believe this to be an entire mistake; for if the tail of a bird could have the slightest effect in guiding, the vane of it must be disposed perpendicularly, and not horizontally, or nearly so, as at present.

" If you cut off the tail of a pigeon, you will find that he can fly and turn perfectly well without it. He may be a little awkward about it at first, but that is because he has lost his balancing power. We all know that it is a common thing to see a sparrow without his tail, therefore, I do not in the least believe that tails have any effect in guiding. They have an important effect in stopping progress, and, undoubtedly, that is one of the necessary elements of turning. If a bird comes close over your head, and is frightened, you will find his claws distended and his tail spread out as a fan, to stop the momentum of his flight. These are the two only observations with which I cannot agree; but as regards the explanation he has given as to the resistance offered by long and narrow wings, he has made an important discovery."

Mr. WENHAM : " With regard to the wing not affording support to the bird during the upward stroke, some of the largest birds move their wings slowly, that is, with a less number than sixty strokes per minute. Now, as a body free to fall must descend fifteen feet in one second, whether in horizontal motion or not, it appears clear to me that there must be some counteracting effect to prevent this fall. When the wing has reached the limit of the down-stroke, it is inclined upwards in the direction of motion, consequently the rush of air caused by the forward speed, weight, and momentum of the bird against the under surface of the wing, supports the weight, even though the wing is rising in the up-stroke at the time. In corroboration of my theory, I will read an extract from Sir George Cayley, who made a large number of experiments. He says, in page 83, of Vol. xxv., 'Nicholson's Journal': — 'The stability in this position, arising from the centre of gravity, being below the point of suspension, is aided by a remarkable circumstance that experiment alone could point out. In very acute angles with the current, it appears that the centre of resistance in the sail does not coincide with the centre of its surface, but is considerably in front of it. As the obliquity of the current decreases, these centres approach and coincide when the current becomes perpendicular to the plane, hence any heel of the machine backwards or forwards removes the centre of support behind or before the point of suspension.'

" From this discovery, it seems remarkable that Sir George Cayley, finding that at high speeds with very oblique incidences the supporting effect became transferred to the front edge, the idea should not have occurred to him that a narrow plane, with its long edge in the direction of motion, would have been equally effective. I may give another illustration. We all know, from our schoolboy experience, that ice which would not be safe to stand upon, is found to be quite strong enough to bear heavy bodies passing over it, so long as rapid motion is kept up, and then it will not even crack. We know, also, that in driving through a marshy part of road, in which you expect the wheels to sink in up to the axles, you may pass over much more easily by increasing the speed. In both these examples there is a greater weight passed over in a given time, and consequently a better support obtained. The ice will not become deflected; neither has the mud time to give way. At a slow speed the same effect may be obtained by extending the breadth of the wheel. Thus, suppose an ordinary wheel to sink ten inches, if you double this width it will sink only five inches; and so on, until by extending the wheel into a long roller you may pass over a quicksand with perfect safety. Now, Nature has carried out this principle in the long wings of birds, and in the albatross it is seen in perfection."

SORCERIES.

A. A Witch.
B. A Spirit raised by the Witch.
C. A Friar raising his Imps.
D. A Fairy Ring.

E. A Witch rideing on the Devill through the Aire.
F. An Inchanted Castle.

Let warlocks grim, an' wither'd hags
Tell how wi' you, on ragweed nags,
They skim the muirs an' dizzy crags
　　Wi' wicked speed,
And in kirk-yards renew their leagues
　　Oure howkit dead.

Burns.

FRANKLIN'S
AERONAUTICAL CORRESPONDENCE.[1]

(*From Sir Joseph Banks to B. Franklin.*)

BALLOONS.

SOHO SQUARE, 13 Sept., 1783.

DEAR SIR: The having it in my power to answer with precision the numerous questions which are asked me by all sorts of people concerning the aerostatic experiment, which, such as they may be, are suggested by every newspaper now printed here, and considered as a part of my duty to answer, is an obligation for which I am indebted to you, and an obligation of no small extent. I lament that the vacation of the Royal Society will not permit me to lay your paper before them as a body immediately; but it shall be the first thing they see when we meet again, as the conciseness and intelligence with which it is drawn up preclude the hopes of anything more satisfactory being received.

Most agreeable are the hopes you give me of continuing to communicate on this most interesting subject. I consider the present day, which has opened a road into the air, as an epoch from whence a rapid increase of the stock of human knowledge must take its date; and that it will have an immediate effect upon the concerns of mankind, greater than anything since the invention of shipping, which opened our way on the face of the water from land to land.

If the rough effort which has been made admits of the improvement that other sciences have received we shall see it used as a counterpoise to absolute gravity, and a broad wheeled wagon travelling with two only, instead of eight horses, the

[1] From *The Works of Benjamin Franklin*, by Jared Sparks, 10 vols., Boston, 1838.

breed of that rival animal in course being diminished, and the human species increased in proportion.

I have thought, as soon as I return from my present banishment, of constructing one and sending it up for the purpose of an electrical kite, a use to which it seems particularly adapted. Be pleased to direct your favors to Soho Square; they are sent to me without delay wherever I am.   Believe me, your obliged, etc.

JOSEPH BANKS.

(From the Same to the Same.)

ASCENT OF A BALLOON.

SOHO SQUARE, 28 Nov., 1783.

DEAR SIR: I am in truth much indebted to you for the favor you have done me in transmitting the copy of the *procès verbal* on Montgolfier's experiment, which I have this moment received.   The experiment becomes now interesting in no small degree.   I laughed when balloons, of scarce more importance than soap bubbles, occupied the attention of France; but when men can with safety pass and do pass more than five miles in the first experiment, I begin to fancy that I espy the hand of the master in the education of the infant of knowledge, which so speedily attains such a degree of maturity, and do not scruple to guess that my old friend, who used to assist me when I was younger, has had some share in the success of this enterprise.

On Tuesday last a miserable taffeta balloon was let loose here under the direction of a Mr. Zambeccari, an Italian nobleman, as I hear.   It was ten feet in diameter, and filled with inflammable air made from the filings of iron and vitriolic acid.   The silk was oiled, the seams covered with tar, and the outside gilt. It had been shown for several days floating about in a public room, at a shilling for the sight, and half a crown for the admission when it should be let loose.

The day was fine; the wind a gentle breeze from the north. At a few minutes after one o'clock it set out, and before night fell at a small village near Petworth in Sussex, having run over about forty-eight miles of country.   The countryman, who first saw it, observed it in its descent.   It appeared at first small, and, increasing fast, surprised him so much that he ran away. He returned, however, and found it burst by the expansion of the contained fluid.

I wish I had somewhat more interesting to tell you of, but I am this moment risen from the dinner, which I annually give to the auditors of the treasurer's account.   I would not delay my thanks to you, and I trust you will make some allowance for the effects of the festivities of the day, which have, I fear, cramped my accuracy; but I can assure you they have not diminished the real gratitude, with which I declare myself your obliged and faithful servant.

JOSEPH BANKS.

(From B. Franklin to John Ingenhousz.)

ON BALLOONS, AND THEIR PROBABLE IMPORTANCE.

PASSY, 16 Jan., 1784.

DEAR FRIEND: I have this day received your favor of the 2d instant.   Every imformation in my power, respecting the balloons, I sent you just before Christmas contained in copies of my letters to Sir Joseph Banks.   There is no secret in the affair, and I make no doubt that a person coming from you would easily obtain a sight of the different balloons of Montgolfier and Charles, with all the instructions wanted; and if you undertake to make one, I think it extremely proper and necessary to send an ingenious man here for that purpose; otherwise, for want of attention to some particular circumstance, or of not being acquainted with it, the experiment might miscarry, which, in an affair of so much public expectation, would have bad consequences, draw upon you a great deal of censure, and affect your reputation.

It is a serious thing to draw out from their affairs all the inhabitants of a great city and its environs, and a disappointment makes them angry.   At Bordeaux lately a person pretended to send up a balloon, and had received money from many people, but not being able to make it rise, the populace were so exasperated that they pulled down his house, and had like to have killed him.

It appears, as you observe, to be a discovery of great importance and what may possibly give a new turn to human affairs. Convincing sovereigns of the folly of wars may, perhaps, be one effect of it, since it will be impracticable for the most potent of them to guard his dominions.   Five thousand balloons, capable of raising two men each, could not cost more than five ships of the line; and where is the prince who can afford so to cover his country with troops for its defence, as that ten thousand men descending from the clouds might not in many places do an infinite deal of mischief before a force could be brought together to repel them?   It is a pity that any national jealousy should, as you imagine it may, have prevented the English from prosecuting the experiment, since they are such ingenious mechanicians, that in their hands it might have made a more rapid progress towards perfection, and all the utility it is capable of affording.

The balloon of Messrs. Charles and Robert was really filled with inflammable air.   The quantity being great it was expensive and tedious filling, requiring two or three days' and nights' constant labor.

It had a *soupape*, or valve, near the top which they could open by pulling a string and thereby let out some air when they had a mind to descend; and they discharged some of their ballast of sand when they would rise again.   A great deal of air must have been let out when they landed so that the loose part might envelop one of them; yet, the car being lightened by that one getting out of it, there was enough left to carry up the other rapidly.   They had no fire with them.   That is used only in M. Montgolfier's globe which is open at the bottom and straw constantly burnt to keep it up.   This kind is sooner and cheaper filled, but must be of much greater dimensions to carry up the same weight, since air rarefied by heat is only twice as light as common air, and inflammable air ten times lighter.   M. Mor-

Plate X.

CARICATURE OF THE ASCENT OF THE FIRST AERIAL TRAVELLERS.
See page 124.

Intentionally blank as was the original edition.

veau, a famous chemist at Dijon, has discovered an inflammable air that will cost only a twenty-fifth part of the price of what is made by oil of vitriol poured on iron filings. They say it is made from sea-coal. Its comparative weight is not mentioned.

I am, as ever, my dear friend,

Yours most affectionately,

B. FRANKLIN.

_____

(*From Francis Hopkinson to B. Franklin.*)

AMERICAN PHILOSOPHICAL SOCIETY. — DEFECTS IN THE USUAL METHODS OF TEACHING LANGUAGES. — BALLOONS.

PHILADELPHIA, 24 May, 1784.

DEAR FRIEND: I cannot suffer so good an opportunity to pass without renewing my assurances of the love and respect I have for you, mine and my father's steady friend.

. . . .

We have been diverting ourselves with raising paper balloons by means of burnt straw, to the great astonishment of the populace. This discovery, like electricity, magnetism, and many other important phenomena, serves for amusement at first; its uses and applications will hereafter unfold themselves. There may be many mechanical means of giving the balloon a progressive motion other than what the current of wind would give it. Perhaps this is as simple as any: Let the balloon be constructed of an oblong form, something like the body of a fish, or of a bird, or a wherry, and let there be a large and light wheel in the stern, vertically mounted. This wheel should consist of many vanes or fans of canvas, whose planes should be considerably inclined with respect to the plane of its motion exactly like the wheel of a smoke-jack. If the navigator turns this wheel swiftly around by means of a winch, there is no doubt but it would (in a calm at least), give the machine a progressive motion upon the same principle that a boat is sculled through the water.

But my paper is almost out and perhaps your patience. If

you can spare time let me know that I live in your remembrance. Any philosophical communications will highly gratify me, and be thankfully received by our society, who expect their president will now and then favor them with his notice. Are we to hope that you will revisit your native country, or not; that country for which you have done and suffered so much? Whilst there is any virtue left in America, the names of Franklin and Washington will be held in the highest esteem. Adieu, and be assured that there is no one who loves you more than your faithful and affectionate

FRANCIS HOPKINSON.

————

(From B. Franklin to Richard Price.)

BALLOONS.— ENGLISH CONSTITUTION. — STATE OF AMERICA.

PASSY, 16 August, 1784.

DEAR FRIEND: I some time since answered your kind letter of July 12th, returning the proof of Mr. Turgot's letter, with the permission of his friends to print it. I hope it came safe to hand. I had before received yours of April, which gave me great pleasure, as it acquainted me with your welfare and that of Dr. Priestley.

The commencement here of the art of flying will, as you observe, be a new epoch. The construction and manner of filling the balloons improve daily. Some of the artists have lately gone to England. It will be well for your philosophers to obtain from them what they know, or you will be behindhand; which in mechanic operations is unusual for Englishmen.

I hope the disagreements in our Royal Society are composed. Quarrels often disgrace both sides; and disputes, even on small matters, often produce quarrels for want of knowing how to differ decently; an art which it is said scarce anybody possesses but yourself and Dr. Priestley.

I had indeed thoughts of visiting England once more, and of enjoying the great pleasure of seeing again my friends there; but my malady, otherwise tolerable, is I find irritated by the

Plate XI.

THE LANDING.

Intentionally blank as was the original edition.

motion in a carriage, and I fear the consequence of such a journey; yet I am not quite resolved against it. I often think of the agreeable evenings I used to pass with that excellent collection of good men, the club at the *London*, and wish to be again among them. Perhaps I may pop in some Thursday evening when they least expect me. You may well believe it very pleasing to me to have Dr. Priestley associated with me among the foreign members of the Academy of Sciences. I had mentioned him upon every vacancy that has happened since my residence here, and the place has never been bestowed more worthily.

.   .   .   .

Many thanks for your kind wishes respecting my health and happiness, which I return fourfold, being ever with the sincerest esteem, my dear friend, your most affectionate

B. FRANKLIN.

(From Richard Price to B. Franklin.)

SINKING FUND. — BALLOONS.

NEWINGTON GREEN, 21 October, 1784.

MY DEAR FRIEND: .   .   .   .

We have at last begun to fly here. Such an ardor prevails that probably we shall soon, in this instance, leave France behind us. Dr. Priestley, in a letter which I have just received from him, tells me that he is eager in pursuing his experiments, and that he has discovered a method of filling the largest balloons with the lighest inflammable air in a very short time and at a very small expense.

.   .   .   .

With the highest regard, I am ever yours,

RICHARD PRICE.

(*To James Bowdoin.*)

DR. JEFFRIES' AERIAL VOYAGE FROM ENGLAND TO FRANCE.

PHILADELPHIA, 1 Jan., 1786.

MY DEAR FRIEND: It gave me great pleasure to receive your kind letter of congratulation as it proved that all my old friends in Boston were not estranged from me by the malevolent misrepresentations of my conduct that had been circulated there, but that one of the most esteemed still retained a regard for me. Indeed, you are now almost the only one left me by nature, death having, since we were last together, deprived me of my dear Cooper, Winthrop, and Quincy.

. . . .

I sent to you by Mr. Gerry, some weeks since, Dr. Jeffries' account of his aerial voyage from England to France which I received from him just before I left that country. In his letter, that came with it, he requests I would not suffer it to be printed, because a copy of it had been put into the hands of Sir Joseph Banks for the Royal Society and was to be read there in November.

. . . .

My acquaintance with Dr. Jeffries began by his bringing me a letter in France, the first through the air, from England. With best wishes of many happy new years to you and good Madam Bowdoin, I have the honor to be, dear Sir, etc.,

B. FRANKLIN.

Plate XII.

EXPERIMENT MADE AT VERSAILLES BY M. MONTGOLFIER, ON THE
19TH OF SEPTEMBER, 1783.

From Des Ballons Aerostatiques, Lausanne, 1784.

Intentionally blank as was the original edition.

A FEW WORDS ABOUT A GREAT HOPE.

THE foregoing Franklin letters show the spirit of their time, and tell, better than any words which can be written at this day, of that great hope which in later years gradually gave way to disappointment. We can hardly wonder that when men first saw the balloon they supposed that the aerial ship of the future had been launched. It must have seemed the most marvellous of all human inventions, and it cannot surprise us that in the Montgolfier decade the flights of men's fancies were taken to heights even dizzier than those reached by their " aerostatic machines."

In our minds the balloon is associated with the gazing multitude at a country fair, and the aeronaut is one of the showmen; but, a century ago, many of those who made ascents were among the most learned men of science, and they risked their lives in singleness of purpose, hoping that they might wrest secrets from dear old Mother Nature, and so add to the sum of human knowledge, which is the sum of human good.

As early as 1766 Henry Cavendish, of England, as a result of his experiments with inflated bladders, stated the specific gravity of inflammable air (hydrogen gas) to be about one-eleventh that of common air.

In November, 1782, at Avignon, France, Stephen Montgolfier caused a silken bag filled with hot air to ascend to the ceiling of his room. A short time after at Annonay, in company with his younger brother Joseph, he repeated the experiment and caused the bag to ascend to a height of about seventy feet.

On the 25th of April, 1783, the same experimenters successfully sent a larger balloon, thirty-five feet in diameter, to a height of about one thousand feet. On the 5th of the following

June, at Annonay, this experiment was repeated "in the presence of a respectable assembly, and a great multitude of people." The balloon is said to have reached a height of six thousand feet. Cavallo says: "This public experiment, recorded with all the accuracy it deserves, was immediately announced to the world; accounts of it were sent to the court of France, to several members of the Academy of Sciences, and almost wherever literary and entertaining correspondence could reach."

On the 27th of August, 1783, the first hydrogen gas balloon was successfully sent up. This was constructed by two brothers of the name of Robert, under the superintendence of M. Charles, professor of natural philosophy in Paris, and afterwards a member of the Academy of Sciences.

The first ascent of living creatures was made at Versailles on the 19th of September, 1783, in the presence of the king, the queen, the court, and an immense number of spectators. The " Boston Magazine " of June and September, 1784, gives an account of the experiment and also the caricatures shown here in Plates X. and XI. The imposing spectacle is more accurately represented in Plate XII. Suspended below the balloon was a cage in which the first aerial travellers were placed, a sheep, a cock, and a duck; according to the magazine just mentioned, " Montgolfier's air balloon having ascended to an amazing height above the clouds and being carried in the air forty-five degrees fell down near a cottage where the poor country people were exceedingly frightened and astonished; the cock, the sheep, and the duck came out of the basket which had been tied to it, unhurt."

The following is quoted from the writings of Mr. James Glaisher, F.R.S.: "The first human being who ascended in a balloon was M. Francois Pilâtre de Rozier, a young naturalist, who two years afterwards was killed in an attempt to cross the English Channel in a balloon. On Oct. 15, 1783, and following days, he made several ascents (generally alone but once with a companion, M. Girond de Villette) in a captive balloon, and demonstrated that there was no difficulty in taking up fuel

Plate XIII

AEROSTATIC MACHINE, 70 FEET IN HEIGHT AND 46 FEET IN DIAMETER,
WHICH ASCENDED FROM PARIS, WITH TWO MEN, TO A HEIGHT
OF 324 FEET, ON THE 19TH OF OCTOBER, 1783.

From Des Ballons Aerostatiques, Lausanne, 1784.

Intentionally blank as was the original edition.

and feeding the fire, which was kindled in a brazier suspended under the balloon, when in the air. The way being thus prepared for aerial navigation, on Nov. 21, 1783, M. Pilâtre de Rozier and the Marquis d'Arlandes first trusted themselves to a free fire balloon. The experiment was made from the Jardin du Chateau de la Muette in the Bois de Boulogne. The machine employed, which was a large fire balloon, was inflated at about two o'clock, and leaving the earth at this time, it rose to a height of about five hundred feet, and passing over the Invalides and the École Militaire, descended beyond the Boulevards, about 9,000 yards from the place of ascent, having been between twenty and twenty-five minutes in the air. The result was completely successful; and it is scarcely necessary to add, the excitement in Paris was very great.

"Only ten days later, viz., on Dec. 1, 1783, MM. Charles and Robert ascended from Paris in a balloon inflated with hydrogen gas."

All this was the beginning of the great hope which has been alluded to. More than a century has gone by, no fulfilment of the hope has come, and now it is the custom to speak of the balloon as a useless thing; *but perhaps we have not yet learned how to use it.* Of course we now know that we cannot drive it against an average wind, yet the ANNUAL ventures the assertion that it is just as unreasonable to speak derisively of the balloon as it would be to comment unfavorably upon a floating dock because of the inability of the latter to win a prize in a yacht race.

Sir John Herschel wrote: "There are epochs in the history of every great operation and in the course of every undertaking to which the coöperations of successive generations of men have contributed (especially such as have received their increments at various and remote periods of history), when it becomes desirable to pause for a while, and, as it were, to take stock; to review the progress made, and estimate the amount of work done; not so much for complacency, as for the purpose of forming a judgment of the efficiency of the methods resorted to, to do it; and to lead us to inquire how they may yet be improved, if such improvement be possible, to accelerate the furtherance of the object, or to ensure the ultimate perfection of its attainments. In scientific, no less than in material and social undertakings, such pauses and *résumés* are eminently useful, and are sometimes forced on our considerations by a conjuncture of circumstances which almost of necessity obliges us to take a *coup d'œil* of the whole subject, and make up our minds, not only as to the validity of what is done, but of the manner in which it has been done, the methods employed, and the direction in which we are henceforth to proceed, and probability of further progress."

If, in our efforts to solve the great problem of aerial navigation, we act in this spirit, we are sure to progress, though, perhaps, because of the great difficulty of our task, we must content ourselves with slow advancement.

LANGLEY'S LAW.

THE following is quoted from the third page of Langley's "Experiments in Aerodynamics:"[1]

"To prevent misapprehension, let me state at the outset that I do not undertake to explain any art of mechanical flight, but to demonstrate experimentally certain propositions in aerodynamics which prove that such flight, under proper direction, is practicable. This being understood, I may state that these researches have led to the result that mechanical sustentation of heavy bodies in the air, combined with very great speeds, is not only possible, but within the reach of mechanical means we actually possess, and that while these researches are, as I have said, not meant to demonstrate the art of guiding such heavy bodies in flight, they do show that we now have the power to sustain and propel them.

" Further than this, these new experiments (and theory, also, when reviewed in their light) show that if in such aerial motion, there be given a plane of fixed size and weight, inclined at such an angle, and moved forward at such a speed, that it shall be sustained in horizontal flight, then the more rapid the motion is, the *less* will be the power required to support and advance it. This statement may, I am aware, present an appearance so paradoxical that the reader may ask himself if he has rightly understood it. To make the meaning quite indubitable, let me repeat it in another form, and say that these experiments show that a definite amount of power so expended at any constant rate, will attain more economical results at high speeds than at low ones, *e.g.*, one horse-power thus employed will transport a larger weight at twenty miles an hour than at ten, a still larger

---

[1] Washington, 1891.

(127)

at forty miles than at twenty, and so on, with an increasing economy of power with each higher speed, up to some remote limit not yet attained in experiment, but probably represented by higher speeds than have as yet been reached in any other mode of transport — a statement which demands and will receive the amplest confirmation later in these pages."

Since Samuel Pierpont Langley has, beyond any question, been the first to discover, to state, and to prove this great law of the economy of high speeds, the editor feels justified in naming it *Langley's Law*.

DARWIN'S OBSERVATIONS.

UNDER the date of April 27, 1834, in his journal[1] kept during the voyage of the "Beagle" round the world, Mr. Darwin, after considering the manner in which vultures[2] find their food, writes as follows:

"Often when lying down to rest on the open plains, on looking upwards I have seen carrion-hawks sailing through the air at a great height. Where the country is level I do not believe a space of the heavens of more than fifteen degrees above the horizon is commonly viewed with any attention by a person either walking or on horseback. If such be the case, and the vulture is on the wing at a height of between three and four thousand feet, before it could come within the range of vision, its distance in a straight line from the beholder's eye would be rather more than two British miles. Might it not thus readily be overlooked? When an animal is killed by the sportsman in a lonely valley, may he not all the while be watched from above by the sharp-sighted bird? And will not the manner of its descent proclaim throughout the district to the whole family of carrion feeders that their prey is at hand?

"When the condors are wheeling in a flock round and round any spot, their flight is beautiful. Except when rising from the ground, I do not recollect ever having seen one of these birds flap its wings. Near Lima, I watched several for nearly half an hour without once taking off my eyes. They moved in large curves, sweeping in circles, descending and ascending without giving a single flap. As they glided close over my head, I

[1] A Naturalist's Voyage. Journal of Researches into the Natural History and Geology of the countries visited during the voyage of H.M.S. "Beagle" round the World. By Charles Darwin, M.A., F.R.S. London. 1845.
[2] Concerning vultures see the writings of L. P. Mouillard mentioned in article on Bibliography on pages 137 and 138 of the ANNUAL.

intently watched from an oblique position the outlines of the separate and great terminal feathers of each wing; and these separate feathers, if there had been the least vibratory movement, would have appeared as if blended together; but they were seen distinct against the blue sky.[1]

" The head and neck were moved frequently, and apparently with force; and the extended wings seemed to form the fulcrum on which the movements of the neck, body, and tail acted. If the bird wished to descend, the wings were for a moment collapsed; and when again expanded with an altered inclination, the momentum gained by the rapid descent seemed to urge the bird upwards with the even and steady movement of a paper kite. In the case of any bird *soaring*, its motion must be sufficiently rapid, so that the action of the inclined surface of its body on the atmosphere may counterbalance its gravity. The force to keep up the momentum of a body moving in a horizontal plane in the air (in which there is so little friction) cannot be great, *and this force is all that is wanted.*[2]

" The movement of the neck and body of the condor, we must suppose, is sufficient for this. However this may be, it is truly wonderful and beautiful to see so great a bird, hour after hour, without any apparent exertion, wheeling and gliding over mountain and river."

---

[1] *Note by the Editor of the* ANNUAL. — Many writers have expressed the opinion that birds which soar with wings apparently motionless derive support, nevertheless, from a vibratory movement of the feathers, and such writers instance the buzzing of the soaring turkey-buzzard as a fact in favor of their theory. Last summer one of my soaring machines had a slight defect in the textile covering of the aerocurves, and when in rapid motion it gave forth a loud buzzing sound, answering quite well to the description which is given of the buzzard's buzzing. I think that a loose feather in a soaring bird's wing would make a similar sound.

[2] These words are italicized by the editor for the purpose of calling attention to the opinion in regard to flight which Darwin held sixty years ago.

WISE UPON HENSON.

THE machine shown in the accompanying plate was patented by Mr. Henson in England in 1842.

Mr. John Wise, in his book entitled "A System of Aeronautics" (Phila., 1850), writes concerning it as follows:

"The next which is worthy of consideration we find in Henson's idea. Many persons in England were sanguine in the belief that his machine was destined to perfect the art of aerial navigation, and it was seriously contemplated to build one after his model, with which to cross the Atlantic. Indeed, it was well calculated to inspire such a belief in the mere theoretical mind, but to the practical man it at once occurs, What is to keep it from tilting over in losing its balance by a flaw of wind, or any other casualty, and thus tumbling to the ground, admitting that it could raise itself up and move forward?

"The principal feature of the invention is the very great expanse of its sustaining planes, which are larger, in proportion to the weight it has to carry, than those of many birds; but if they had been still greater, they would not have sufficed of themselves to sustain their own weight, to say nothing of their machinery and cargo; surely, though slowly, they would have come to the ground. The machine advances with its front edge a little raised; the effect of which is to present its under surface to the air over which it is passing, the resistance of which, acting on it like a strong wind on the sails of a windmill, prevents the descent of the machine and its burden. The sustaining of the whole, therefore, depends upon the speed at which it is travelling through the air, and the angle at which its under surface impinges on the air in its front; and this is exactly the principle by which birds are upheld in their flight with but slight motion of their wings, and often with none.

" But, then, this result, after the start, depends entirely on keeping up the speed, and there remains beyond that, the still more formidable difficulty of first obtaining that speed. All former attempts of this kind have failed, because no engine existed that was at once light enough and powerful enough to lift even its own weight through the air with the necessary rapidity. Mr. Henson has removed this difficulty, partly by inventing a steam-engine of extreme lightness and efficiency, and partly by another and very singular device, which requires particular notice. The machine, fully prepared for flight, is started from the top of an inclined plane, in descending which it attains a velocity necessary to sustain it in its further progress. That velocity would be gradually destroyed by the resistance of the air to the forward flight; it is, therefore, the office of the steam-engine and the vanes it actuates simply to repair the loss of velocity; it is made, therefore, only of the power and weight necessary for that small effect. Here, we apprehend, is the chief, but not the only merit and originality of Mr. Henson's invention; and to this happy thought we shall probably be indebted for the first successful attempt to traverse at will another domain of nature."

In the "Popular Science Review," 1869, Vol. VIII., p. 1, Mr. F. W. Brearey states that this machine was never constructed.[1]

The account of it is given in this ANNUAL partly because of the interest which attaches to Mr. Henson's plans on account of their date, and partly for the sake of showing what Mr. Wise thought of the combination of an aeroplane with a steam-engine.

Nine years after the publication of his book, Mr. Wise with John La Mountain made one of the most famous balloon voyages on record. They left St. Louis on July 1, 1859; "the States of Illinois and Indiana were passed over in the night and Ohio was reached in the morning. The balloon then passed across Lake Erie into New York, and to Lake Ontario, into

---

[1] See " Progress in Flying Machines," Chanute, p. 84.

Plate **XIV.**

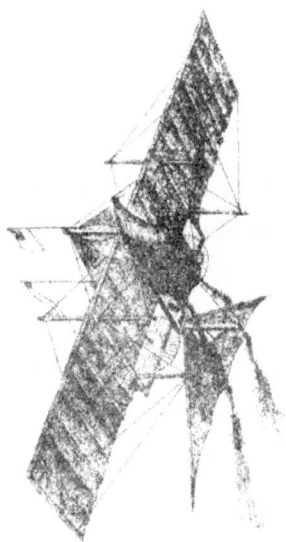

HENSON'S PROJECTED FLYING MACHINE. 1842.

Intentionally blank as was the original edition.

which it descended, but rose again, and a landing was made in Henderson, Jefferson County, N.Y. The time occupied in making this journey was nineteen hours and fifty minutes, and the distance traversed 1,150 miles, or 826 in an air line." [1]

Twenty years later, in 1879, Mr. Wise again ascended from St. Louis, this time in the " Pathfinder." He was last seen to pass over Illinois in a northeasterly direction, and is supposed to have perished in Lake Michigan. James Glaisher wrote of him: " In America Mr. Wise is *par excellence* the aeronaut; he has made several hundred ascents, and many of them are distinguished for much skill and daring. He also appears to have pursued his profession with more energy and capacity than has any other aeronaut in recent times, and his ' History of Aerostation ' shows him to possess much higher scientific attainments than balloonists usually have. In fact, Mr. Wise stands alone in this respect, as nearly all professional aeronauts are destitute of scientific knowledge."

---

[1] Appleton's Cyclopædia of American Biography, Vol. III., p. 602. See also Vol. VI., p. 581.

TABLE OF WIND VELOCITIES,

FOR THE YEAR 1892.

•

Compiled from the Report of the Chief of the Weather Bureau, 1891-92.

MAXIMUM VELOCITIES ARE FOR A FIVE–MINUTE PERIOD. A WIND VELOCITY OF 40 MILES PER HOUR IS CONSIDERED A GALE.

	Average for the year. Miles per hour.	Maximum monthly average. Miles per hour.	Minimum monthly average. Miles per hour.	Maximum velocity.	Number of days with gales.
Boston, Mass..........	12.0	15.9 in March.	9.6 in July.	48	8
Buffalo, N.Y.	10.9	13.7 in December.	8.4 in August.	55	26
Chattanooga, Tenn. ...	5.1	7.5 in April.	3.4 in September.	35	0
Chicago, Ill...........	16.8	22.2 in April.	13.2 in June.	72	59
Cleveland, O..........	11.1	15.6 in November.	8.2 in March.	64	16
Denver, Col.	7.4	9.1 in April.	5.3 in February.	48	3
New Orleans, La.	8.8	12.0 in April.	6.0 in August.	50	5
New York, N.Y.	10.8	14.6 in March.	6.9 in August.	49	6
Pittsburgh, Pa.........	6.5	8.4 in November.	4.6 in July.	38	0
Portland, Me..........	8.4	10.9 in March.	7.2 in August.	45	4
Portland, Ore.........	6.0	9.2 in November.	4.6 in January.	41	2
St. Louis, Mo.	11.0	13.4 in January.	8.1 in August.	48	13
San Francisco, Cal.....	8.7	12.0 in July.	4.5 in January.	60	6
Savannah, Ga.	7.8	9.0 in April.	6.2 in August.	32	0

Plate XV.

LA MINERVE. *vaisseau aérien destiné aux découvertes par le professeur Robertson*

Die Minerva, ein Luftschiff welches durch Professor Robertson zu einer Entdeckung bestimt ist

CARICATURE FROM ASTRA CASTRA.   LONDON, 1865.

Reference notes not given.

Intentionally blank as was the original edition.

BIBLIOGRAPHY OF AERONAUTICS.

As stated in the opening article, the earliest written records of the study of natural and artificial flight are to be found in the MSS. of Leonardo da Vinci. The following-named work contains all that has so far been published concerning the master's researches in this direction: *I MANOSCRITTI DI LEONARDO DA VINCE. CODICE SUL VOLO DEGLI UCCELLI, e varie altre materie pubblicato da Teodoro Sabachnikoff. Transcrizioni e note di Giovanni Piumati Traduzione in Lingua Francese di Carlo Ravaisson-Mollieu. PARIGI, EDOARDO ROUVEYRE EDITORE.* MDCCCXCIII.

A list containing the names of publications dating from 1627 to 1865, more than seventy-five in number, is to be found on pp. 463–464 of *Astra Castra, Experiments and Adventures in the Atmosphere*, by Hatton Turnor. London, 1865. The compiler designates seventeen of these works by an asterisk, and states in a foot-note that "These books are at the service of the public in the library of the Patent Office, Southampton Buildings, E.C."

Among the seventeen is the following: 1855, *George James Norman : Aeronautica Illustratica, a Complete Cabinet of Aerial Ascents and Descents, from the Earliest Periods to the Present Time.* 10 large folio vols. London.

In a note Mr. Turnor says: "The cost of making this collection exceeded £300. It was twice sold by auction, and bought the second time for the library of the Patent Office for £26. The collector is a young man in somewhat distressed circumstances. To his industry the author owes the greater part of his own collection, as they were the duplicates that necessarily accumulate in so extensive a collection."

Among the rarer works which the editor of the ANNUAL has in his collection are the following:

Des Ballons Aérostatiques,[1] *de la Manière de les Construire, de les faire élever: avec quelques vues pour les vendre utiles.* Lausanne, 1784.

An Account of the First Aerial Voyage in England ; with autograph. By Vincent Lunardi, Esq. London, 1784.

The History and Practice of Aerostation. By Tiberius Cavallo, F.R.S. London, 1785.

A Treatise upon Aerostatic Machines. By John Southern. Birmingham, 1785.

An Account of Five Aerial Voyages in Scotland.[1] By Vincent Lunardi, Esq. London, 1786.

A Journal of Natural Philosophy, Chemistry and the Arts. By William Nicholson. 35 vols. London, 1802 to 1813.

A System of Aeronautics, comprehending its earliest investigations, and modern practice and art. Designed as a history for the common reader, and guide to the student of the art. In three parts. Containing an account of the various attempts in the art of flying by artificial means from the earliest period down to the discovery of the aeronautic machine by the Montgolfiers, in 1782, and to a later period.

With a brief history of the author's fifteen years' experience in aerial voyages. Also, full instructions in the art of making balloons, parachutes, etc., etc., as adapted to the practice of aerial navigation, and directions to prepare experimental balloons. By John Wise, Aeronaut. 13 plates, 310 pp. Philadelphia, 1850.

Reports of the Aeronautical Society of Great Britain. One to twenty-three, in twenty-one parts. Eighteenth and nineteenth reports in one part; twentieth and twenty-first reports in one part. London, 1866–1893. See lists of publications given in the above.

The best of the world's knowledge of aeronautics is to be found in the two thousand pages of these reports. The organization has never been a large one, and probably years will pass by before the importance of its twenty-nine years of work will be fully understood and appreciated. Even as the missal

---

1 Kindly given by Dr. J. R. C.

painters kept art alive during the Dark Ages, so has this band of men kept aeronautics alive during the years in which their branch of science has been by the many regarded almost as a pseudo-science. The editor wishes to make the fullest acknowledgment of the debt he owes to this society.

On the Various Modes of Flight in Relation to Aeronautics. By Dr. James Bell Pettigrew. A paper read before the Royal Institution of Great Britain, March 22, 1867. See also *Animal Locomotion; or Walking, Swimming and Flying.* By the same author. No. 8 in the International Scientific Series. 130 illustrations. $1.75. Appleton, New York.

Animal Mechanism. A treatise on terrestrial and aerial locomotion. By E. J. Marey, Professor at the College of France. No. 11 in the International Scientific Series. 117 illustrations. $1.75. Appleton, New York.

Aerial Navigation. By the late Charles Blachford Mansfield, M.A. Edited by his brother, Robert Blachford Mansfield, with a preface by J. M. Ludlow. London, 1877.

Aerial Navigation. By Edmund Clarence Stedman. Century Magazine, New York, 1879.

The Empire of the Air. By L. P. Mouillard. 66 pp. In Annual Report of the Board of Regents of the Smithsonian Institution to July, 1892. Washington, 1893 Original published in Paris in 1881.

Experiments in Aerodynamics. By Samuel Pierpont Langley. This memoir (No. 801, Smithsonian Series) forms part of Volume XXVII., Smithsonian Contributions to Knowledge. Washington, 1891.

This monumental work is so well known that it needs no notice here.

Aerial Navigation. By Octave Chanute, C.E. 36 pp. New York, 1891.

The Possibility of Mechanical Flight. By S. P. Langley. Century Magazine, New York, September, 1891.

Aerial Navigation. The Power Required. By Hiram S. Maxim. Century Magazine, New York, October, 1891.

The Aeroplane. By Hiram S. Maxim. The Cosmopolitan Magazine, New York, June, 1892.

Aerial Navigation. By John P. Holland. The Cosmopolitan Magazine, New York, November, 1892.

Aeronautics. A monthly journal. 12 numbers. October, 1893–September, 1894. Containing papers read at the Chicago Conference on Aerial Navigation, and other valuable matter. M. N. Forney, editor and proprietor, 47 Cedar street, New York.

American Engineer and Railroad Journal. Monthly. This publication devotes several pages of each issue to the subject of aeronautics. The publisher states that Mr. O. Chanute, C.E., of Chicago, has consented to act as associate editor of this department, and will be a frequent contributor to it. Those who are fortunate enough to be familiar with the work which Mr. Chanute has done in the past will need no further words to awaken their interest in this publication. Price, 25 cents per copy, $3.00 annual subscription. M. N. Forney, publisher, 47 Cedar street, New York.

Engineering News. New York. In the columns of this paper the editor, Mr. A. M. Wellington, has printed valuable matter concerning the mechanics of flight. See the issue of Oct. 12, 1893, *et seq.* It is regretted that a lack of complete files of this paper make a more extended notice impossible at this time.

The Internal Work of the Wind. By Samuel Pierpont Langley. Published by the Smithsonian Institution, Washington, 1893.

Zeitschrift für Luftschiffahrt und Physic der Atmosphere. By Otto Lilienthal. Berlin, 1894.

The Maxim Air-Ship. An interview with the inventor. By H. J. W. Dam. McClure's Magazine, New York, January, 1894.

Gliding Flight. By L. P. Mouillard. Cosmopolitan Magazine, New York, February, 1894.

New Lights on the Problem of Flying. By Prof. Joseph LeConte. The Popular Science Monthly, New York, April, 1894.

Progress in Flying Machines. By Octave Chanute, C.E. 308 pp., 85 illustrations. $2.50. Published by the American Engineer and Railroad Journal, 47 Cedar street, New York, 1894. "A history of the efforts that have been made to solve the problem of aerial flight, from the first recorded experiments to the present time." The appendix contains Herr Lilienthal's own account of his 1893 experiments.

This book is one of the most important which has ever been published touching the problem of aerial navigation.

Contents. — General Principles. — Wings and Parachutes. — Screws to Lift and Propel. — Aeroplanes (177 pp.). — Conclusion. — Appendix.

The Development of Aerial Navigation. By Hiram S. Maxim. The North American Review, New York, September, 1894.

The Flying Man. Otto Lilienthal's Flying Machine, by Vernon. Illus. McClure's Magazine, New York, September, 1894.

The Evolution of a Flying Machine. By Hiram S. Maxim. A paper read before the Mechanical Science Section of the British Association, at Oxford, Aug. 10, 1894. Reprinted in the Boston Evening Transcript, Sept. 8, 1894.

Aerial Navigation. By A. F. Zahm, of Johns Hopkins University. Pph., 32 pp. A lecture delivered before the Franklin Institute, Jan. 5, 1894. Philadelphia, 1894.

Aerial Navigation. By J. G. W. Fijnje van Salverda. Translated from the Dutch by George E. Waring, Jr. New York, 1894, Appleton.

Teoria del volo e della navigazione aera. By A. Faccioli. 8vo. Milano, 1894.

THE ROC.

From Lane's Arabian Nights. London, 1853.

Plate XVI.

A GLIMPSE OF THE FUTURE.

From Astra Castra. London, 1865.

Intentionally blank as was the original edition.

[Reprint of a pamphlet published in January, 1894.]

THE

PROBLEM OF MANFLIGHT.

BY

JAMES MEANS

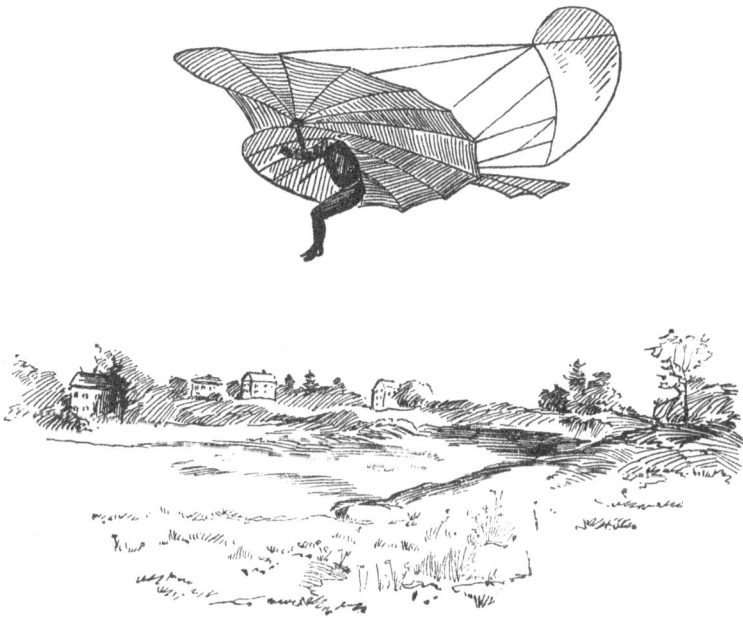

THE FLIGHT OF OTTO LILIENTHAL, OF STEGLITZ, PRUSSIA, AS ACTUALLY
ACCOMPLISHED IN 1893. ACCURATELY DRAWN FROM
AN INSTANTANEOUS PHOTOGRAPH.

BOSTON, MASS.:

W. B. CLARKE & CO.,

340 WASHINGTON STREET.

1894.

(141)

Intentionally blank as was the original edition.

THE PROBLEM OF MANFLIGHT.

As the century draws to its close the interest in the subject of aeronautics steadily increases. There already exists a keen curiosity to know what the aerial machine of the future is likely to resemble, and also to know whether the nineteenth or the twentieth century will claim it for its own.

In the present article the writer wishes to show what inferences may be drawn from the laws of nature as so far ascertained by observation and experiment, and he wishes also to point out a way which may lead to further progress.

The investigators of this subject are now divided into two camps : on the one side there are men who, like Mr. Maxim, are endeavoring to construct machines which will carry motors and therefore be self-propelling ; on the other side there are men like Mr. A. M. Wellington, who maintains that a motor is unnecessary and that wind-power is sufficient.

In the New York Engineering News, of Oct. 12, 1893, Mr. Wellington, in a very interesting article entitled " The Mechanics of Flight," makes the following statement : "If the conclusions so far reached in this paper be accepted, it is obvious that they greatly simplify the problem of artificial flight by reducing to a minimum the demand for power, making it chiefly necessary for acquiring the first initial velocity. All attempts at aviation which include any motor for pro-

pulsion are, in my judgment, on wrong lines, and pre-
destined to certain failure, since they not only neglect,
but destroy, the action of the forces by which true flight
may be and is attained.   I will not go so far as to say
that some (soaring) birds, in the exuberance of power,
may not use the wings to accelerate, as they do to retard
motion.   I think they do, but only in an abnormal way;
it is wholly unnecessary, and even destructive of all
normal flight.   The fish needs a propeller, because it
has no gravity in water; the bird does not need it,
because it has gravity, and in that gravity has the best
and smoothest of all conceivable means of propulsion, if
he can make the wind lift him uphill whenever he has
slid far enough downhill.   If so, man commits an ab-
surdity when he flies in the face of nature and assumes
a propelling force where none is needed or exists."

Later on in this article, I wish to describe an instrument, experiments with which can be made to answer
for us the question as to whether or not a motor is
needed; but just here further quotations should be given
to show the trend of the best thought.

Aeronautics (N.Y.) for January contains Professor
Langley's remarkable paper entitled "The Internal
Work of the Wind."   The closing paragraph is as
follows:

"The final application of these principles to the art
of aerodromics seems, then, to be, that while it is not
likely that the perfected aerodrome (air-runner) will
ever be able to dispense altogether with the ability to
rely at intervals on some internal source of power, it
will not be indispensable that this aerodrome of the
future shall, in order to go any distance — even to cir-
cumnavigate the globe without alighting, — need to carry
a weight of fuel which would enable it to perform this

journey under conditions analogous to those of a steam-ship, but that the fuel and weight need only be such as to enable it to take care of itself in exceptional moments of calm."

Mr. Octave Chanute, in his admirable chronicle entitled "Progress in Flying-Machines," which will soon be published, says in one of his closing chapters: "But it is possible to utilize a still lighter power [than that of engines], for we have seen that the wind may be availed of under favorable circumstances, and that it will furnish an extraneous motor which costs nothing and imposes no weight upon the apparatus.

"Just how much power can be thus utilized cannot well be told in advance of experiment; but we have calculated that under certain supposed conditions it may be as much as some six-horse power for an aeroplane with one thousand square feet of sustaining surface; and we have also seen that while but few experimenters have resorted to the wind as a motor, those few have accomplished remarkable results."

The indications seem to be that we must try to construct a machine analogous to the sailing-yacht rather than to the steamship, though perhaps the aerial machine of the future will be, so far as power is concerned, analogous to the yacht Sunbeam with its auxiliary screw.

Before continuing further with this subject, I wish to call attention to certain facts concerning the storage of power and the flight of soaring birds. First, in regard to the storage of power. It is well known that the construction of a useful electric storage-battery presents a most difficult problem. Such a storage device is needed for use upon the surface of the earth; yet, for purposes of aerial navigation, there is a much simpler accumulator

which can be used. Take, for example, one hundred
pounds of lead and let energy be stored in it by giving
it altitude, just as energy is stored in the weight of a
clock when it is wound.

What is known as one-horse power is the amount of
energy which must be exerted in lifting thirty-three
thousand pounds at the rate of one foot per minute, or
five hundred and fifty pounds at the rate of one foot per
second, or fifty-five pounds at the rate of ten feet per
second. To give an illustration, it may be stated that if
a man weighing one hundred and sixty-five pounds
ascends a flight of steps ten feet high in three seconds,
he exerts for the time being just one standard horse-
power.

A small balloon which can lift one hundred pounds
of lead three hundred and thirty feet high in one minute
exerts one-horse power.

The lead when lifted to this height has stored within
itself thirty-three thousand foot-pounds of energy.

Now, if weights can be made to slide downhill upon
aeroplanes at very gentle grades, then the balloon becomes a valuable motor which stores energy in its load
by giving it altitude, and the weight lifted becomes a
reservoir of the very power needed for its own transportation, and the name of Montgolfier, the inventor of
the under-estimated balloon, takes its place as that of the
real founder of the useful art of aerial transportation.

Whether or not it is possible to transport freight by
sliding it down long and gentle inclines by means of
aeroplanes will be considered further on; just here we
must consider the soaring power of birds.

In "The Reign of Law," by the Duke of Argyll (first
published in 1867), there is a most notable chapter in
which the flight of birds is analyzed. In a note the

author makes the following statement: " I owe to my father [John, seventh Duke of Argyll] my knowledge of the theory of flight, which is expounded in this chapter. The retired life he led, and the dislike he had of the work of literary composition, confined the knowledge of his views within a comparatively narrow circle. But his love of mechanical science, and his study of the problem during many years of investigation and experiment, made him thoroughly master of the subject."

Every student of the subject of flight should read the interesting work just mentioned. We may not agree with all the conclusions which are reached, yet the author gives most stimulating food for thought.

The following paragraphs are among the most striking, showing, as they do, advanced ideas:

" In the first place, it is remarkable that the force which seems so adverse — the force of gravitation drawing down all bodies to the earth — is the very force which is the principal one concerned in flight, and without which flight would be impossible. It is curious how completely this has been forgotten in almost all human attempts to navigate the air. Birds are not lighter than the air, but immensely heavier. If they were lighter than the air they might float, but they could not fly. This is the difference between a bird and a balloon." (p. 130, Am. ed.)

. . . .

" No bird is ever for an instant of time lighter than the air in which it flies ; but being, on the contrary, always greatly heavier, it keeps possession of a force capable of supplying momentum, and therefore capable of overcoming any lesser force, such as the ordinary resistance of the atmosphere, and even heavy gales of wind. The force of gravitation, therefore, is used in

the flight of birds as one of the most essential of the
forces which are available for the accomplishment of the
end in view." (p. 131.)

. . . .

"The lightness of a bird is a limit to its velocity.
The heavier a bird is, the greater is its possible velocity
of flight — because the greater is the store of force ;
or, to use the language of modern physics, the greater is
the quantity of 'potential energy' which, with proper
implements to act upon aerial resistance, it can always
convert into upward, or horizontal, or downward motion,
according to its own management and desires." (p.
144.)

. . . .

"When a strong current of air strikes against the
wings of a bird, the same sustaining effect is produced
as when the wing strikes against the air. Consequently
birds with very long wings have this great advantage,
that, with pre-acquired momentum, they can often for
a long time fly without flapping their wings at all.
Under these circumstances a bird is sustained very
much as a boy's kite is sustained in the air. The string
which the boy holds, and by which he pulls the kite
downwards with a certain force, performs for the kite
the same offices which its own weight and balance and
momentum perform for the bird. The great long-
winged oceanic birds often appear to float rather than
to fly. The stronger is the gale, their flight, though less
rapid, is all the more easy, so easy indeed as to appear
buoyant ; because the blasts which strike against their
wings are enough to sustain the bird with comparatively
little exertion of its own, except that of holding the
wing vanes stretched and exposed at proper angles to
the wind. And whenever the onward force previously

acquired by flapping becomes at length exhausted, and the ceaseless, inexorable force of gravity is beginning to overcome it, the bird again rises by a few easy and gentle half-strokes of the wing. Very often the same effect is produced by allowing the force of gravity to act, and when the downward momentum has brought the bird close to the ground or to the sea, that force is again converted into an ascending impetus by a change in the angle at which the wing is exposed to the wind." (p. 152.)

It is to be regretted that the limits of this article prevent more extended quotations from this remarkable book.

Now let us recall what we have seen at sea.

When one stands on the after-deck of a steamer in crossing the ocean, he may watch the soaring gulls to his heart's content. When the ship struggles painfully to force her way into the teeth of a gale, the birds make sport for themselves — they rise and dip, thus conquering the wind. How? Simply by *tacking;* in one sense, just as a yacht tacks to windward. Neither bird nor yacht can sail into the eye of the wind by the wind's power, but either can, by use of that power, reach an objective point lying to windward.

But here the reader may say that the parallelism between the bird and the sailing craft is not correctly drawn, because the yacht has a keel immersed in a dense medium which resists and prevents the making of leeway.

Yet the soaring bird has something which, at necessary times, holds it against the wind just as effectually as the keel holds the yacht: that something is *momentum,* which, while it lasts, holds the bird against the wind as firmly as the kite-string holds the boy's kite.

In Fig. 1, let S represent a steamship going eastward at the rate of twenty miles per hour; W the

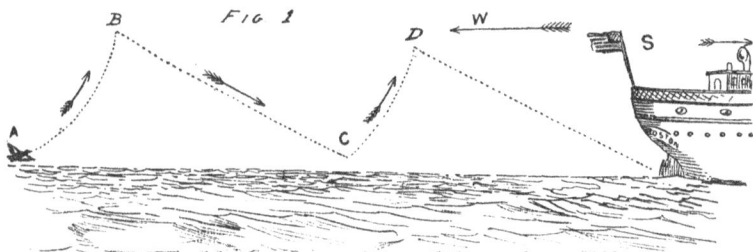

wind blowing westward at the rate of twenty miles per
hour; A a gull near the water's surface, with momentum which for the instant gives him an eastward
velocity of twenty miles per hour. While the bird's
momentum lasts it holds him firmly against the wind.
At the point A the bird inclines his wings so that the
wind strikes them on the under side, and he is lifted and
lifted until, at the point B, his momentum is so reduced
that he must tack; then he gives to the wind the thin
edge of his wings and slides down to the point C, and
then, with velocity regained, he repeats the manœuvre.
Altitude sacrificed becomes velocity or momentum, and
momentum sacrificed becomes altitude.   In this description of the gull's soaring to windward, the movement is reduced to its simplest elements, and it leaves
out of account the graceful sinuosity of the bird's airy
travels, just as the teacher of dancing leaves grace out
of account when she teaches the beginner the elements
of the steps.

What has here been said about the storage of energy
in weights, and concerning the elements of flight, is all
intended to lead up to the important subject of sliding

freight downhill upon aeroplanes. It may be asked, How about a calm?

There is no calm for the aeroplane. Give it altitude and it can gain velocity, and velocity gives the *wind of flight*.

The plan for the transportation of freight is simply this: at each shipping-point a power-house (D, Fig. 2)

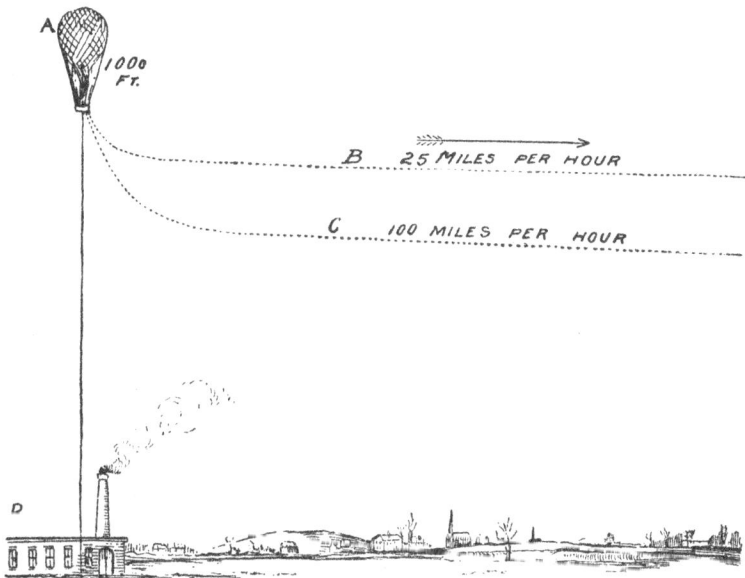

Fig. 2.

may be established to operate captive balloons. These should be cellular, and should be made to hold gas with little waste. In its action the apparatus would be what might be called an inverted elevator; that is, the steam or water-motor in the power-house would not hoist the freight, but, instead, would pull the balloon down after *it* had hoisted the freight and discharged it by means of a soaring machine, which will presently be described.

In Fig. 2 A represents a captive balloon at a height
of one thousand feet.   B and C represent the courses
which would be taken by dirigible aeroplanes or soaring machines bearing loads of freight.

Perhaps this seems fanciful.   Then let it be remembered that the feat of safely sliding down a long and
gentle incline upon an aeroplane has already been performed by Otto Lilienthal, of Steglitz, Prussia.   His
experiments were illustrated and described in the Berlin
Illustrirte Zeitung of Oct. 7, 1893, and one of the drawings — all of which were correctly made from instantaneous photographs — is here reproduced on the first
page of cover.   An improvement upon Lilienthal's
device may be made by adding a pendulum. *

*Now, in order to travel long distances in the air
it is only necessary to improve the dirigibility of the
aeroplane so that the angle of descent can be brought
to a minimum.*

How can this be done?   By making repeated experiments with very simple and inexpensive mechanical contrivances called soaring machines, these to be
dropped from a height.

In Fig. 2 it will be noticed that the course marked B
indicates a speed of twenty-five miles per hour, that
marked C a speed of one hundred miles per hour.

What speed may we expect of an improved soaring-
machine? and upon how gentle a decline can we hope
to see it maintain its initial velocity?   First, note the
fact that with a dirigible aeroplane or soaring machine
the rate of speed is practically a matter of choice and
depends at the start upon the length of the first swoop.
The limit of speed will probably be decided by the

* See U. S. Letters Pat. No. 376937.

strength of the machine and the breathing requirements of the aerial pilot. Let us consider a railroad train. Man has safely travelled at a rate of one hundred and twelve miles per hour. On May 11, 1893, the Empire State express on the N.Y.C. R.R. reached that speed in a mile run in thirty-two seconds, one mile westward from Crittenden. So we know that man can safely breathe when travelling at over one hundred miles per hour; yet for this, of course, he needs the same protection which a cab gives to the locomotive engineer.

We will answer as well as we may the second question, Upon how gentle a decline may we hope to see an aerial machine maintain its initial velocity? When a railway car is at rest upon a smooth steel track having a down grade of one and twenty-three one-hundredths feet in every one hundred feet, it will remain at rest if undisturbed; but let it be once started downward by ever so slight an impulse and it will run down the track, gaining velocity to the end of the grade. It encounters the head resistance of the air and the friction of the track, but an aerial machine would encounter only air-resistance; is it not, therefore, reasonable to suppose that a dirigible aeroplane would in a calm, maintain its initial velocity while running upon a down grade of air of one foot in every one hundred feet? If so, an altitude of ten or twelve hundred feet would send a soaring machine eighteen or twenty miles, and greater altitudes would give longer flights, if, as may be supposed, the rarefaction of the air can be offset by an increase of velocity. These are surmises, but the way to learn is to experiment with soaring machines.

It is above all things important that a soaring machine should, when desired, automatically keep itself in a horizontal or slightly descending course. I have this winter begun a series of experiments with soaring machines, and when these are finished the full details will be reported.

In November, 1893, I launched several of these machines from the balcony of the tower of Boston Light, and more recently I have experimented from the top of the cliffs at Manomet. The former place is an ideal one for the purpose of experiment, being as it is, one hundred and eleven feet above the sea with a straight drop of seventy or eighty feet. Unfortunately, a gale of wind was blowing when I visited the light, and two out of the three machines were total failures, being badly bent by the wind before they were launched. The third machine righted itself before reaching the ground, but the pendulum, which will presently be described, was too light to do efficient work.

The experiments from the cliffs at Manomet were even less successful, owing to the fact that the descent is not sheer. All of the machines failed to gain sufficient velocity to clear the cliff.

Those who wish to experiment with machines weighing only a few pounds will probably find that a height of seventy or eighty feet will be sufficient if the position gives a straight drop. When it comes to experimenting with a soaring machine as large as Lilienthal's and carrying a weight representing that of a man, the summit of Mt. Willard, near the Crawford House, N.H., will be found an excellent place.

To any one who desires to take up this most fascinating study, Figs. 3 and 4 will give a general idea as to the construction of his first instrument for making experiments. A represents a backbone five-eighths of an inch square and four feet long, made of pine wood; B, the main aeroplane, eight inches wide and three feet

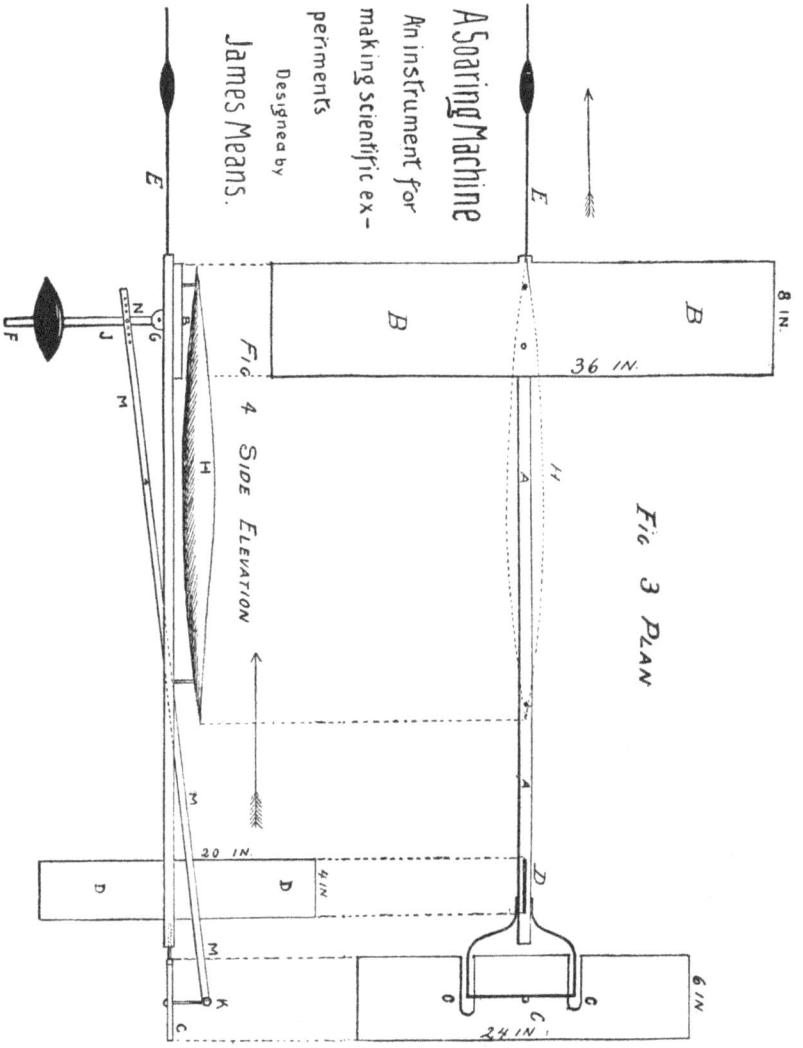

A Soaring Machine

An instrument for making scientific experiments

Designed by

James Means.

Fig 3 Plan

8 IN

36 IN.

B

E

Fig 4 Side Elevation

20 IN.

4 IN

D

24 IN.

6 IN

long. This should be made of light tin plate, and bent
in the middle so as to form a flattened V; the angle
should be about one hundred and seventy degrees.
C represents a steering aeroplane six inches by twenty-
four inches, pivoted at cc, also made of light tin plate;
D, a vertical aeroplane four inches by twenty inches,
rigidly fixed in the wooden backbone; E, a rod of
steel wire, eighteen or twenty inches long, and carrying
an adjustable leaden weight of three ounces; K, a rod
two and one-half inches long, soldered in the centre of
and vertical to the plane C, with a pivot at the upper
end with which the rod MM is connected. This rod
should have five or six pivot-holes at its forward end N,
so that its working length may be varied for different
experiments; J, a rod pivoted at G, free to swing fore
and aft; N, a pivot where the rod MM joins the rod J;
F, a leaden weight adjustable higher or lower upon the
rod J; its proper weight is x, an unknown quantity.
Upon ascertaining by repeated experiment the right
weight for F, the right *position* for the adjustable
weight E, and the right *length* for the rod MM, the reaching of the maximum efficiency of a system of aeroplanes
largely depends.   I think that this sets forth with clearness the problem as it stands to-day.   When it is fully
solved — and it certainly seems solvable — right and left
steering will be a less difficult matter, and alighting
will be accomplished by killing the momentum when
near the ground by an abrupt upward slant of the main
aeroplanes; but this is an anticipation and a digression.
Now to return to the instrument we are considering:
this soaring machine is intended to gain velocity by a
swoop, and then automatically steer itself into a horizontal or very slightly descending course, as indicated
by B and C in Fig. 2.   It depends upon the principle

that the pendulum rod always seeks the perpendicular;
for instance, when the machine is launched pointing
steeply downward, the positions of the pendulum and
aeroplanes are as shown in Fig. 5; therefore the steering aeroplane C will, as soon as velocity is gained, lay

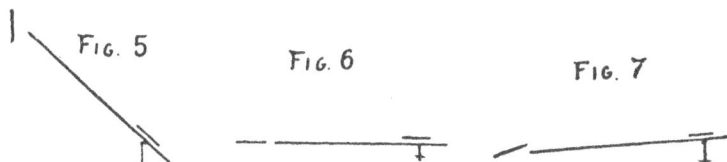

FIG. 5   FIG. 6   FIG. 7

a strong hold upon the wind of flight, and have a tendency to bring the machine into a horizontal course.
Now, if the length of the rod MM is made correct by
adjustment at the pivot-holes near N, when the desired
course, a very gentle decline, is reached, both aeroplanes will be approximately horizontal, as shown in
Fig. 6. If, however, the machine deviates either
upward or downward from its intended course, the
weight at the end of the pendulum causes the steering
aeroplane to correct the error. Fig. 7 shows the
effect of a slight upward deviation.

H represents a long and very slender air-recepta-
cle made of thin rubber and inflated; this should be
pointed at both ends. It may be used to keep the
machine afloat when experiments are made near the
water. I have not yet used this, but have allowed my
machines to go to pieces. The design here given calls
for aero*planes* as being more easily made than aero-
curves modelled after the wings of birds, but in all
probability the latter will eventually displace the former.

We are brought now, after this consideration of the
greatest mechanical problem of the age, to ask, What

shall be done to bring to our own century the credit and honor of reaching the solution?

The answer is, encourage experiments with soaring machines. Have regattas and large prizes. Appeal to the people's love of sport, and show what possibilities of recreation have been suggested by the experiments of Otto Lilienthal. Tobogganing on ice we can have only a few weeks in the year: tobogganing on air is possible at all seasons. When we have made our aeroplanes or aerocurves automatic in their steering action, flights like Lilienthal's will be, to say the least, no more dangerous than football and quite as interesting.

In order to encourage the designing and construction of soaring machines, I suggest that a sum of money be raised to be offered as a prize to the constructor of the most successful soaring-machine, the award to be made after a public trial of the same, to take place early in September of the present year (1894).

I will subscribe one hundred dollars if others will subscribe, in any sums they choose, nine hundred dollars more, to make a purse of one thousand dollars, provided that the publisher of some journal of wide influence will be custodian of the fund.

One or two more thoughts in conclusion. We have seen how the soaring bird tacks, first up, then down, then up again, and then down again. That conveys the idea of the perfection of rapid transit for passengers and freight. With the captive balloon we can tack up, with the soaring machine we can tack down. Short tacks up, long tacks down; there is no calm for the aeroplane; give it altitude and it can seize from the calm the wind of flight.

Imagine a bowling alley four hundred feet long, perfectly level, with an athlete at one end and a boy at the other. Let the chute which returns the balls have a drop of fifteen inches in every one hundred feet; imagine the game to be one of rapid transit instead of tenpins. It is a competition between the two ends of the alley to see which end can make the most of what energy it has. Let the athlete exert all his strength to propel the spheres; see them arrive at the end of the alley after their journey of four hundred feet, with sluggish speed; the boy lifts them to a height of five feet to the chute, gives them a gentle push, and they are returned to the athlete's end, arriving, not as sluggards, but as filled with energy. A short tack up and a long tack down is what does it.

There you have the old and the new methods of transit represented. The athlete represents the steam locomotive which, with all its polish and glitter, wastes energy. The boy represents the balloon, the lifter, which stores energy in matter by giving it altitude. The chute represents the free highway which through all the centuries men have supposed to be lacking.

Aerial transit will be accomplished because the air is a solid if you hit it hard enough.

EDITORIAL.

SINCE the foregoing pamphlet was published, about a year ago, I have become more than ever firmly convinced that the soaring-machine is, of all others, the instrument by which we must, for the present, acquire knowledge.

With all due respect to those who are constructing machines to start along the ground with motors, I still express the opinion that such machines are less instructive than are soaring-machines launched from considerable heights. The reason is this. The art of steering machines of the former kind has only been partially acquired, consequently long flights of such do not occur, and their conduct can be studied for a very brief time only. But the soaring-machine, with the potential energy of lead for its motor, when launched from a captive balloon at a considerable height, must, of necessity, declare itself for a considerable length of time and teach the observer new things with every new flight. Every movement is instructive to the designer, and no hasty wreck can occur to deprive him of the opportunity for study. When a soaring-machine which will carry four or five hundred pounds of lead or sand-bags has been satisfactorily designed, then will it be time to consider motors. To trust valuable motors to machines before we have successfully carried sand-bags uses up appropriations faster than is necessary.

After the soaring-machine is sufficiently improved, the adding of a motor — if such be found necessary — will be the adding of a new force which will tend to throw the machine out of equilibrium; yet the power can be applied very gradually so that we may learn to counteract the disturbance of the equilibrium which it causes.

SIR GEORGE CAYLEY made what he called his "noble white bird,"[1] but unfortunately, so far as known, he left no mechanical drawing with dimensions and weights. Had he included such a drawing in his published articles, it would have been a help to later investigators. Since Sir George's day there have been many accounts published of the performances of soaring devices, but most of these fail to give the detailed drawings with weights and dimensions which are needed to give to such accounts their highest value to workers.

On page 163 of Mr. Chanute's "Progress in Flying Machines" there will be seen a cut of a soaring device invented by William Beeson and patented in 1888. Automatic longitudinal stability is intended to be secured by a pendulum, the rod of which always seeks the perpendicular. I quote from Mr. Chanute's book: "Mr. Beeson states in his patent that 'this machine is self-supporting in a light wind, say, of ten miles or more per hour, and that when once raised by a kite or otherwise, and cut loose, it will of itself perform the evolutions of a soaring bird and rise to any altitude.'"

Mr. Chanute continues, "The writer confesses that he has tried the experiment with a small model and has failed; and so, in the hope that some of his readers may be more fortunate, he has given the account of what seems to be a remarkably simple device — if it will work."

I have given several months of study to this pendulum, and have made a large number of experiments with machines working upon this principle. In May, 1894, I went again to Manomet Cliffs provided with six machines of the type shown in Fig. 1.

Owing to the limited height of the place of launching, — less than one hundred feet, — only a short swoop was possible, and the velocity necessary to carry heavy weights could not be obtained.

With wings four feet from tip to tip and six inches wide, the weight of lead used on the pendulum was only twelve ounces. The best flight obtained in this instance was with one instrument

---

[1] See page 25.

which, after swooping to within about twenty-five feet of the
beach, went to windward in a nearly horizontal course, a distance
of about two hundred feet, before alighting.   In this case there
was no apparent unsteadiness caused by the oscillation of the
pendulum.   In other trials a tendency of the pendulum to oscil-

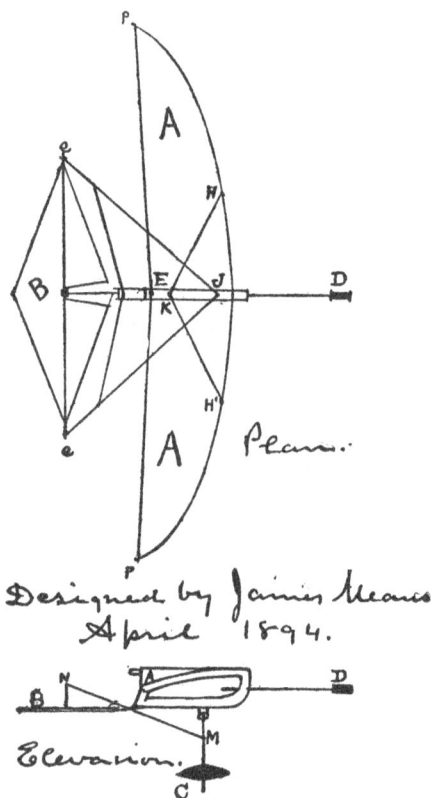

Figure 1.

AA, main aerocurves. B, a plane moving upon the axis ee. C, a weigh
movable up or down upon the pendulum rod. MN, a connecting rod pivoted at
each end and made so that its length is easily varied. D, a movable head-
weight. EJ, wooden support for metal frame.

When this machine is in horizontal flight, if the front tips up or down, the
pendulum rod in seeking the perpendicular inclines the plane B in a direction
which steers the machine back into its horizontal course.

late was shown. I am of the opinion that the best results which can be obtained with a pendulum, when used in a machine of this type, will be when it is so confined by stops that the amplitude of its swing is made small, and perhaps even then a dash-pot may be necessary to give additional steadiness to the pendulum.

During the summer of the present year (1894) I spent the greater part of my time in working at the bench and in the field. I made experiments at York Harbor, Maine, with soaring-machines having rudders acting upon the principle advocated by Alphonse Pénaud in 1872.[1]

These were raised to a height by means of large kites,[2] and were suspended from the kite-string at a distance of 100 to 150 feet from the kite. Fig. 2 shows a very simple device which I used to secure the release of my machines at any desired moment. If my progress during the summer was slow it was largely owing to the fact that calms and light winds were so prevalent that oftentimes I could not get more than three or four days in a month when the wind was sufficient to lift my weights.

In order to launch machines from a greater height than my kites had carried them during the summer I went in September to the summit of Mt. Willard, in the White Mountains. There being at that place a precipitous descent of 800 to 900 feet, I hoped for good results. I went provided with twenty instruments all ready to put together. After trials of seven or eight of these I found that most of them were caught by eddies of wind which turned them in and wrecked them against the face of the cliff. The remaining instruments I still hold, hoping at some future time to launch them from a captive balloon. I believe that to be the most satisfactory way of experimenting with motorless instruments.

The flights of my soaring-machines during the past months have been sometimes downward, sometimes erratic, and some-

---

[1] See "Progress in Flying Machines," pps. 117, 118, and "Report of Aeronautical Society of Great Britain, 1874.

[2] I wish to express my thanks to Mr. William A. Eddy, of Bayonne, N.J., for his kindness in sending me a working drawing of a tailless kite of his own design.

times approximately horizontal; in watching their conduct I
have not learned how to make an entirely satisfactory machine,
yet I believe that I have gained some ideas which may have
value in determining future methods of experimental work.
Knowing of no source of information such as I have needed,
my apparatus and methods have been of the crudest kind.

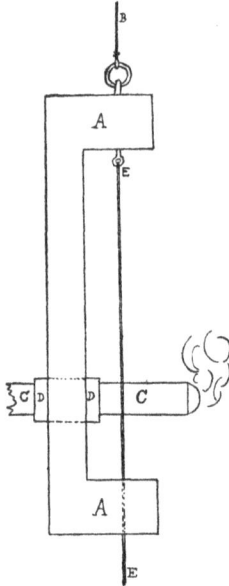

Figure 2.

AA, a block of pine wood 5 in. long ¾ inch thick. *B*, string attached to kite
string. *CC*, a slow-match. *DD*, a strip of spring sheet-brass rolled over a pencil
into a cylinder which binds the slow-match slightly so that the latter may be moved
back and forth. *EE*, the string which sustains a soaring-machine. Small slow-
match in ordinary winds burns about ⅛ of an inch per minute. By adjusting the
length of the match the string will be cut when desired.

Having altered my design after every trial, I can now offer to
experimenters the drawing of an instrument which will, I think,
be useful to them in beginning a series of investigations. It
involves no new principle, but as the result of experiment it is
proportioned in such a way that it will soar *instructively*.

Whatever the merits or the faults of the design may be, its
dimensions are given, and any one may test it. (See Fig. 3.)

I wish to give to those who are just beginning to experiment, a warning against an error by the commission of which I have been retarded in work. In a series of experiments, slight changes only should be attempted in the design. Frequently a favorable flight will lead one to carry a supposed improvement so far that total failure results. The study cannot be successful unless most careful observations are made to ascertain what causes produce what effects.

The effects of slight changes can be traced to their causes; it is otherwise with the effects of radical changes.

A DEFINITE PLAN. — If I were asked what is the thing to be done which will most help us toward the full solution of the great problem, I should answer, carry out the idea advanced in May, 1890, by Mr. Octave Chanute, and organize an American Aeronautical Society.

Such a society should have for its prime object the encouragement of experimental work. It should offer prizes for the most effective soaring-machines, and every summer it should establish, for a week or two, a camp in some secluded place where competitive trials of soaring or flying machines could be had. An aeronaut should be engaged to keep a captive balloon in the air during the working hours of each day. By a simple hoisting-apparatus attached to the car of the balloon the instruments to be tested could be raised to any desired height and released at will. Thus long flights could be surely attained, and every instrument would necessarily fully declare itself before reaching the ground.

There would at first be many machines which would be failures, but no one need hesitate because of publicity. Each machine could be entered by number, and a working drawing of it placed on file, and the onlookers need not know the name of the designer in case he should wish to remain unknown.

I fully believe that if Mr. Chanute were to carry out his idea (fixing the annual assessment at a sum not exceeding one or two dollars), that a strong and useful working organization could be built up.

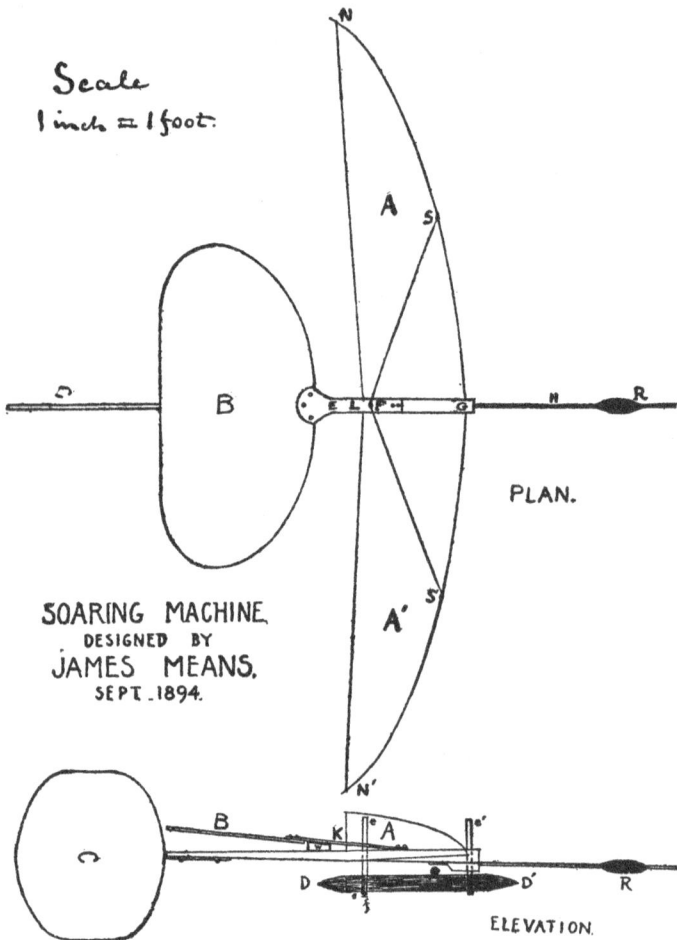

Scale
1 inch = 1 foot.

A

S

B

R

PLAN.

SOARING MACHINE
DESIGNED BY
JAMES MEANS,
SEPT. 1894.

A'

S

N'

B

K

A

D   D'   R

ELEVATION.

Figure 3.

Materials. — I have found the following excellent: For aeroplanes, the stiffest and flattest Japanese fans that can be had. For aerocurves, varnished silk. For frames, paragon umbrella-ribs. These give remarkable strength for their size and weight. When a wing is made flat, of silk and steel, being elastic, it becomes in action an aerocurve, concaved on the under side. For ballast-carriers, pieces of bamboo, to which are fitted conical plugs of wood. For ballast, lead or sand.

AA', main aerocurves. B, aeroplane to keep the machine in a horizontal course. C, vertical aeroplane to keep the machine headed into the wind. DD', ballast-carrier, which may be moved forward or aft when the binding screw f is loosened; ee', rods sliding up and down in the wooden backbone FG, thus raising or lowering the ballast-carrier. R, a leaden weight which slides on the rod H. K, a flat piece of spring steel which carries the aeroplane B; this spring is fastened to the wooden backbone by two stout screws. It tends to press very strongly upon the wedge W. When the wedge W is moved backward or forward it changes the angle of the aeroplane B relatively to the aerocurves AA.

The main aerocurves, in order to give lateral stability to the machine, are inclined to each other at an angle of about 165°, according to the principle explained by Sir George Cayley on page 30.

In using umbrella ribs, the braces which run to the umbrella handle should not be detached, as these and their pivots come just where they are needed to give strength to the soaring-machine. S and S' are the points of junction; you will find holes in the braces at F; through these a clinching nail can be driven. From N to L and from N' to L are taut cords; these pull in the tips of the ribs and give just the right curve to the forward edges.

Given the positions and areas of surface as per the scale of the drawing, it will be seen that in the adjustment of this machine for the nearest possible approach to automatic horizontal flight there are three factors concerned, namely:

1. The total weight of ballast.
2. The angle of plane B[1].
3. The position of the centre of gravity.

This machine is designed for the express purpose of ascertaining the best possible combination of factors. It will make its first flight instructively with two pounds of ballast, with the centre of gravity at the point indicated by the black dot, and with the plane B at the angle shown in the drawing. Taking the result of this flight as a starting-point, the machine is capable of improvement to an indefinite extent.

---

[1] See description of the Pénaud rudder, on p. 56 of the Ninth Annual Report of Aeronautical Society of Great Britain.

FOR several winters past I have been watching the soaring gulls from my back window, and I have repeatedly observed one phenomenon which leads to the thought that there is some property in air which still remains a profound mystery, and that in the future this very property, whatever it may be, will be found to be one of the most important factors in explaining flight. What I refer to is this: we know that when an aeroplane or an artificial wing is *swiftly* moved against the wind, or the wind against it, there is a strong upward thrust; but I have repeatedly seen the gull over glassy water — indicating a calm — move horizontally, with fixed wings, with *such extreme slowness* that the act seems to be against all the known laws of nature.

SINCE the year 1790 there have been issued by the United States Patent Office one hundred and forty-nine patents for aerial machines or parts of the same. The writer has the drawings and specifications of these bound in a single volume. A study of this inclines one to think that the successful flying-machine of the future will be in its main features, not a new invention, but merely a new design. So many patents have been issued for various combinations of aeroplanes and screws and for wings of different kinds, that in future it will probably be the task of the designer to properly proportion and arrange the parts, and for the inventor to improve the details.

For one example: the aeroplane machine with screw propulsion and with ground wheels for starting was patented in the United States so long ago that the patent has now expired. The invention is public property, but so far as now known a full-sized machine of this sort has never been properly designed, and the problem of securing its dirigibility has not been solved. While undirigible, it is of no practical use, and just as there is no royal road to skating, so there is no method of learning to steer aerial machines save the experimental one.

ONE thing is certain: if the problem of flight had been fully solved by some one unknown to us, and if that person were to present us with a perfect flying-apparatus, that instrument would be of no more immediate use to us than the latest safety bicycle would be to the king of Dahomey, or a pair of skates to a man who had never seen ice. Bicycling, skating, walking, swimming, and flying are all movements which must be learned by practice if at all, and, moreover, the process of learning is, in each case, likely to be attended with some personal discomfort.

MAXIM speaks of Lilienthal as a parachutist, and likens him to a flying-squirrel.[1] He also says that his (Lilienthal's) experiments do not assist us at all in performing actual dynamical flight.

Lilienthal, after alluding to the unwieldiness of Maxim's machine, says, "After all, the result of his labors has only been to show us ' how not to do it.' "[2]

If any two men should be friends rather than foes, these are the two. Each has certain ideas and qualifications which the other lacks, and it is the greatest of pities that they cannot clasp hands over the watery channel.

THE present revival of interest in the subject of aeronautics leads many writers to confidently predict a solution of the great problem at an early date; yet I venture to say that the more one studies the subject the more plainly he sees the enormous difficulties which are still unconquered, and the more inclined he is to think that many years will elapse before any travelling in the air becomes an important feature in the daily life of the human race. Yet these very difficulties are what give the subject its extreme fascination.

IN flying a tandem of ten or twelve kites upon a single string one gets an inkling of the erraticalness of wind passing over land. Wind is the queerest stuff conceivable. Over land,

[1] See Maxim's communication to the Boston "Transcript" of Sept. 8, 1894.
[2] See "The American Engineer," New York, Dec. 1894, p. 576.

especially over broken land, it is absolutely unlike the sailor's wind. Over trees and hillocks it is often broken into billows and eddies great and small, and it often rolls over and over itself as do the great breakers on a long beach.

IF some manufacturer of bicycles would cause one such machine to be built with an aerial screw for propulsion he would furnish a valuable instrument for experimental purposes.

WRITERS frequently express the opinion that aerial machines when they come into use will first be applied to the purposes of warfare. I venture to predict otherwise. It seems likely that the earliest use of aerial machines will be for purposes of sport, and most interesting sport it will be.

The second use will, I think, be to bring ore down from hundreds of mines where it would never pay to run cables. The ore has the energy of position; it is all ready to slide down from the mountains if it is given a smooth road of air upon which to slide. Men who are now earning moderate pay as trapeze performers seem to have the requisite coolness, quickness, and muscular skill to learn the art of steering ore-carrying aeroplanes as Lilienthal steers his machine down a gentle incline. Probably the wages of gold-carrying aerial pilots would be higher than those of trapeze performers.

WHEN we try, by the exercise of our imagination, to peer into the future and see the successful air-ships in their swift action, we probably err if we limit our imaginings to a single type.

The investigator who has given most of his thought to aeroplane machines propelled by screws, naturally in his flights of fancy sees the perfected type of such patrolling the airy spaces. The one who has most carefully watched the soaring birds of prey sees man with wings and the faculty of using them. The advocate of brute force sees no wing-like aeroplanes, but only a machine with whirring steel screws boring into the air in flight or hovering as the colossal pterodactyl might have hovered if he had had the anatomy and the method of the humming-bird. Perhaps in time all of these fancies may be justified by the same multiformity in aerial vessels which now prevails in marine craft. Is the idea far-fetched? We must judge by the past. Let us go back to the simplest forms of water vehicles. The cake of ice upon which the polar bear is carried by a strong and favoring breeze to the shore under his lee; the floating log which sustains the early descendant of the anthropoid apes; the hollowed log, the dug-out, paddled by the savage who has begun to think a little; the dug-out with a bush for a sail used by the savage who begins to take an interest in labor-saving devices; the birch canoe of the American Indian, so wonderful in adaptation to all the needs which brought it into existence — directly from these, what has come? Small boats with oars and sails, galleys with oars, caravels with sails, every kind of paddling, rowing, sailing, electric, and steaming craft, and, leading them all, impressive to the last degree, as she breasts the Atlantic gale of a winter's night, the " Lucania," the *fin-de-siècle* flower.

No one dares to set a limit to man's achievements; we are now only in the earliest stages of the science of aerial navigation; our descendants may see in air-ships the multiformity which we now see in marine craft. There are probably many more ways than one to solve the great problem, if only we can find them out.

SWIFT at the scourge the ethereal coursers fly,
While the smooth chariot cuts the liquid sky.
Heaven's gates. spontaneous open to the powers,
Heaven's golden gates, kept by the winged hours;
Commission'd in alternate watch they stand,
The sun's bright portals and the skies command,
Involve in clouds the eternal gates of day,
Or the dark barrier roll with ease away.
The sounding hinges ring: on either side
The gloomy volumes, pierced with light, divide.
The chariot mounts, where deep in ambient skies,
Confused, Olympus' hundred heads arise ;
Where far apart the Thunderer fills his throne,
O'er all the gods superior and alone.
There with her snowy hand the queen restrains
The fiery steeds, and thus to Jove complains:

.   .   .   .

To whom assenting, thus the Thunderer said :
" Go! and the great Minerva be thy aid.
To tame the monster-god Minerva knows,
And oft afflicts his brutal breast with woes."
He said ; Saturnia, ardent to obey,
Lash'd her white steeds along the aërial way.
Swift down the steep of heaven the chariot rolls,
Between the expanded earth and starry poles.
Far as a shepherd from some point on high,
O'er the wide main extends his boundless eye ;
Through such a space of air, with thundering sound,
At every leap the immortal coursers bound :
Troy now they reach'd and touch'd those banks divine,
Where silver Simoïs and Scamander join.
There Juno stopp'd, and (her fair steeds unloosed)
Of air condensed a vapour circumfused :
For these impregnate with celestial dew,
On Simoïs brink ambrosial herbage grew.
Thence to relieve the fainting Argive throng,
Smooth as the sailing doves they glide along.

The Iliad of Homer.   Book V.   Pope.

FINIS.

www.ingramcontent.com/pod-product-compliance
Lightning Source LLC
Chambersburg PA
CBHW031254090426
42742CB00007B/454